Algebra

Best Value Books™

Table Of Contents

About the book...

This book is just one in our Best Value™ series of reproducible, skill oriented activity books. Each book is developmentally appropriate and contains over 100 pages packed with educationally sound classroom-tested activities. Each book also contains free skill cards and resource pages filled with extended activity ideas.

The activities in this book have been developed to help students master the basic skills necessary to succeed in mathematics. The activities have been sequenced to help insure successful completion of the assigned tasks, thus building positive self-esteem as well as the self-confidence students need to meet academic and social challenges.

The activities may be used by themselves, as supplemental activities, or as enrichment material for the mathematics program.

Developed by teachers and tested by students, we never lost sight of the fact that if students don't stay motivated and involved, they will never truly grasp the skills being taught on a cognitive level.

About the author...

Dawn Talluto Jacobi holds a Bachelor's degree in Mathematics. While raising her three children (Eric, Kaitlin, and Matthew) Dawn found herself in demand as math tutor. She noted a common thread that kept children from finding success in math class - the lack of self-confidence. Dawn developed a game format that attracted and held her students' attention because it made math more fun. Dawn discovered that she enjoyed teaching and decided to enter the field full time. She is currently teaching high school Algebra and is working on her Master's degree in Education.

Senior Editors: Patricia Pedigo and Roger DeSanti
Production Director: Homer Desrochers
Production: Arlene Evitts and Debra Ollier

Solving Equations

You must always have a "goal" in mind when you approach a math problem. whenever you are faced with the situation of solving an equation (whether it is a simple equation or a complicated equation), always remember: (If the variable is alone on one side of the equation sign, the answer will be all alone on the other side.)

Your goal will always be: **Variable = Answer**

Use these steps to help you solve equations.

1) Simplify parenthesis using the distributive property.

2) Combine like terms independently on each side of the equation

3) Move all variables to the left side of the equation by using addition and subtraction.

4) Move all numbers to the right side of the equation using addition and subtraction.

5) Simplify with multiplication and division.

Exponents

$x^2 = x \cdot x$ x is the base 2 is the exponent

$xa \cdot xb = xa+b$ If you have the <u>same</u> base, just add the exponents.

$(x^a)^b = x^{a \cdot b}$ If you raise a power to a power, just multiply exponents.

$\dfrac{x^a}{x^b} = x^{a-b}$ When dividing expressions with the same base, just subtract the exponents.

$x^{-a} = \dfrac{1}{x^a}$ Negative exponents mean you must take the reciprocal of the expression.

$(xy)^a = x^a y^a$ All terms in parenthesis share the exponent.

     CD-3732

Factoring $x^2 + bx + c$

To factor an expression, use these methods as they are ordered.

I GCF   Greatest Common Factor
   Example: $6x + 6y = 6(x + y)$
   Example: $2x^2 + 4x = 2x(x + 2)$

II DOTS   Difference Of Two Squares
   $a^2 - b^2 = (a + b)(a - b)$
   Example: $3x^2 - 27 = 3(x^2 - 9) = 3(x + 3)(x - 3)$
   Example: $x^2 - 121 = (x + 11)(x - 11)$

III FOIL   First Outer Inner Last
   Let the addition and subtraction signs "guide" your factoring.
   First, in your problem, look at the **second** sign:
   If second sign is positive then use same signs in factors
   If second sign is negative use different signs in factors
   Second, in your problem look at the first sign:

If second sign is positive	If first sign is positive, then both signs in factoring will be positive. Example: $x^2 + 7x \oplus 10$ (second sign positive) $x^2 \oplus 7x + 10$ (first sign positive) $(x \oplus 2)(x \oplus 5)$ (both signs positive)	If first sign is negative, then both signs in factoring will be negative. Example: $x^2 - 7x \oplus 10$ (second sign positive) $x^2 \ominus 7x + 10$ (first sign negative) $(x \ominus 2)(x \ominus 5)$ (both signs negative)
If second sign is negative	If first sign is negative, then sign of larger factor will be negative. Example: $x^2 - 3x \ominus 10$ (second sign negative) $x^2 \ominus 3x + 10$ (first sign negative) $(x \ominus 5)(x \oplus 2)$ (larger factor negative)	If first sign is positive, then sign of larger factor will be positive. Example: $x^2 + 3x \ominus 10$ (second sign negative) $x^2 \oplus 3x - 10$ (first sign positive) $(x \oplus 5)(x \ominus 2)$ (larger factor positive)

Operations on the Real Numbers

Integers
The integers are ...,-4, -3, -2, -1, 0, 1, 2, 3, 4,...
As you can see, there are three dots before and after the list of integers. This means that there is no largest integer or smallest integer.

On a number line, the integers to the right of zero are **positive integers** and the integers to the left of zero are the **negative integers**. Zero is neither a positive integer or a negative integer.

The **natural numbers** are all positive integers.
$$1,2,3,4,....$$
The **whole numbers** consist of all of the positive integers and zero.
$$0,1,2,3,4,....$$

A **variable** is a letter of the alphabet that is used in mathematics to stand for a number. For example, in the problem $2t = 10$, t is the variable.

The quotient of two integers is a **rational number.** A rational number can be written as $\frac{x}{y}$, in the case that x and y are integers and y is not equal to zero ($y \neq 0$). A rational number written this way is called a fraction.

Every integer is a rational number. A number written as a decimal, such as 3.5, is also a rational number.

All rational numbers can be written as a repeating or terminating decimal.

An **irrational number** is a number whose decimal expansion does not terminate and never repeats. For example $\pi = 3.141592604...$

The **rational numbers** and the **irrational numbers** make up the **real numbers**.

Patterns

French mathmetician Blaise Pascal developed a triangular pattern to describe the coefficients for the expansion of (a + b) , for consecutive values of "n" in rows. In the triangular formation below, note that (a + b)^0 = 1 and (a + b)^1 = a + b.

Part A. Directions: In Pascal's triangle below, fill in the blanks to extend the pattern.

```
n = 0                          1
n = 1                        1   1
n = 2                      1   2   1
n = 3                    1   3   3   1
n = 4                  1   __   6   __   __
n = 5                __   __   __   10   __   __
n = 6              __   __   __   __   __   __   __
n = 7            __   __   __   __   __   __   __   __
n = 8          __   __   __   __   __   __   __   __   __
n = 9        __   __   __   __   __   __   __   __   __   __
```

Part B. For the problems below, use Pascal's triangle to find the coefficients of the expansion (a + b).

1. (a + b)^3 = ___a^3 + ___a^{2}b + ___ab^2 + ___b^3

2. (a + b)^6 = ___ a^6 + ___a^{5}b + ___a^{4}b^2 + ___a^{3}b^3 + ___a^{2}b^4
         + ___ab^5 + ___b^6

3. (a + b)^4 = ___a^4 + ___a^{3}b + ___a^{2}b^2 + ___ab^3 + ___b^4

4. (a + b)^7 = ___a^7 + ___a^{6}b + ___a^{5}b^2 + ___a^{4}b^3 + ___a^{3}b^4 + ___a^{2}b^5
         + ___ab^6 + ___b^7

Patterns

Carefully study the patterns of numbers below. Complete each pattern.

1. 10, 100, 1,000, 10,000, _____, _____, _____.

2. 17, 15, 25, 23, 33, 31, _____, _____, _____, _____.

3. 800, 80, 8, 0.8, 0.08, _____, _____, _____, _____.

4. 1, 4, 9, 16, 25, _____, _____, _____, _____, _____.

5. 1, 6. 5, 10, 9, 14, 13, _____, _____, _____, _____.

6. $\dfrac{1}{2}$, $\dfrac{2}{3}$, $\dfrac{3}{4}$, $\dfrac{4}{5}$, $\dfrac{5}{6}$, $\dfrac{6}{7}$, _____, _____, _____, _____.

7. 7, 21, 63, 189, _____, _____, _____, _____.

8. 125, 120, 115, 110, _____, _____, _____, _____.

9. 3, 6, 7, 14, 15, 30, 31, _____, _____, _____, _____.

10. 2, 20, 4, 40, 8, 80, 16, _____, _____, _____, _____.

CHALLENGE! The following is a special pattern called the Fibonacci sequence. See if you can discover and complete this interesting pattern.

1, 1, 2, 3, 5, 8, 13, _____, _____, _____, _____, _____.

The Addition of Real Numbers

$$-8 + 5 = -3$$

Add.

1. $8 + (-7)$

2. $-55 + -8 + -4 + 54$

3. $-21 + 12 + -1 + -19$

4. $3 + 12 + -13 + 36$

5. $18 + 21 + (-3) + 9$

6. $9 + 7 + -7 + -9$

7. $12 + 7 + -16 + 9 + -34$

8. $2.7 + (-4.8)$

9. $8.3 + (3.9)$

10. $5.8 + 8.4$

11. $-5\frac{3}{4} + (-2\frac{3}{4}) + 8$

12. $3\frac{5}{8} + (-1\frac{2}{3}) + 2$

13. $3\frac{3}{5} + 4\frac{3}{7}$

14. $-3\frac{1}{6} + (-9\frac{3}{12}) + 6$

15. $2.76 + -6.56 + -9.72$

16. $3.45 + 2.65 + -9.43$

17. $-2\frac{3}{5} + (-5\frac{3}{7}) + 3$

18. $-8\frac{3}{5} + 3\frac{3}{7}$

19. $3.54 + 4.27 + 7.43$

20. $7.867 + -5.329$

The Addition of Real Numbers

$$-12 + 4 = -8$$

Add.

1. $2 + 5 + -3$

2. $12 + -9 + 17$

3. $34 + -13 + -8 + 0 + 34$

4. $21 + 3 + -9 + 22$

5. $21 + 9 + (-6) + 7$

6. $3 + (-3) + 4 + (-5)$

7. $2 + -5 + -5 + 2$

8. $3.6 + (-2.5) + -5.5$

9. $(-.6) + -.56 + 3$

10. $2.2 + -3.4 + 5.1$

11. $-6\frac{2}{5} + (-3\frac{2}{5}) + 7$

12. $2\frac{3}{5} + (-3\frac{2}{5}) + -6$

13. $2\frac{1}{2} + 6\frac{1}{2}$

14. $-2\frac{1}{3} + (-5\frac{7}{10}) + -7$

15. $8.43 + -9.98 + -3.23$

16. $2.54 + -5.21 + -6.34$

17. $-1\frac{2}{3} + (-3\frac{3}{5}) + 4$

18. $-7\frac{2}{4} + 2\frac{3}{4}$

19. $2.54 + -5.87 + -32.65$

20. $4.983 + 5.342$

The Subtraction of Real Numbers

$$9 - (-2) = 9 + 2 = 11$$

Subtract.

1. $45 - 129$

2. $18 - (-13)$

3. $-201 - (-42)$

4. $38 - 39 - (-13)$

5. $9 - (-2) - 8 - 7$

6. $35 - 67 - 85 - 21 - 12$

7. $12 - 7 - (-16) - 9 - (-34)$

8. $0 - 21$

9. $9 - (-32)$

10. $-34 - 6$

11. $-\frac{3}{5} - \frac{2}{4} - (-\frac{4}{5})$

12. $-\frac{4}{7} - \frac{1}{3} - (\frac{2}{3})$

13. $\frac{3}{5} - \frac{5}{8}$

14. $9.432 - 4.348 - 32.938$

15. $3.9 - 5.9$

16. $3.434 - 9.294$

17. $8 - (-12)$

18. $9 - 3.8$

19. $2.19 - 7.8 - 8.31$

20. $-7 - (-2)$

The Subtraction of Real Numbers

$$8 - (-3) = 8 + 3 = 11$$

Subtract.

1. $232 - 45$

2. $23 - (-21)$

3. $321 - (-34)$

4. $245 - 32 - (-36)$

5. $8 - (-5) - 7 - 9$

6. $43 - 78 - 35 - 21$

7. $66 - 35 - 74 - 32$

8. $-45 - 0$

9. $4 - (-8)$

10. $-19 - 8$

11. $-\frac{2}{3} - \frac{1}{3} - (-\frac{1}{3})$

12. $-\frac{4}{5} - \frac{1}{2} - (\frac{2}{5})$

13. $\frac{2}{3} - \frac{4}{5}$

14. $2.456 - 4.345 - 5.457$

15. $4.3 - 7.6$

16. $4.346 - .4537$

17. $7 - (-22)$

18. $4 - 3.8$

19. $5.34 - 9.9 - 3.65$

20. $-9 - (-6)$

The Multiplication of Real Numbers

(-3) (-4) = 12

Multiply.

1. -9 • 12

2. (4) (8)

3. (12) (-3) (4)

4. (0) (2) (-213)

5. (-5) (-5) (-5)

6. (-3) (-9)

7. (-3) (0)

8. 12 (-3)

9. (7) (-9) (-12)

10. (5) (2) (-1)

11. (21.2) (-3.95)

12. (7.56) (3.2) (4.3)

13. (2.22) (-1.11)

14. 6(23)

15. $(-\frac{2}{3})$ (-1.6)

16. $(-\frac{5}{9})$ (9.9)

17. $(-\frac{3}{5})$ $(\frac{3}{5})$

18. $(-\frac{4}{5})$ (2.2)

19. (2.4) (-1.4)

20. -7 (-7)

The Division of Real Numbers

$$7 \div 3.5 = 2$$

Divide.

1. $-47 \div 7$

2. $45 \div (-8)$

3. $-36 \div (4)$

4. $65 \div 15$

5. $0 \div (-8)$

6. $520 \div (0)$

7. $\dfrac{36}{6}$

8. $\dfrac{105}{5}$

9. $\dfrac{102}{17}$

10. $\dfrac{54}{-9}$

11. $(6.8) \div (-2.4)$

12. $-72 \div (9)$

13. $(-12) \div (9.9)$

14. $(-56) \div (8.0)$

15. $\left(-\dfrac{2}{3}\right) \div (-18)$

16. $\left(-\dfrac{4}{5}\right) \div (-1.6)$

17. $\left(-\dfrac{3}{5}\right) \div \left(\dfrac{3}{5}\right)$

18. $\left(-\dfrac{4}{6}\right) \div (36)$

19. $(-3.4) \div (-9.99)$

20. $-21 \div (-9)$

Order of Operations

When solving an equation, be sure to follow the **priority pyramid**.

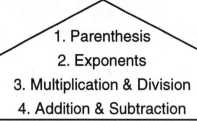

1. Parenthesis
2. Exponents
3. Multiplication & Division
4. Addition & Subtraction

Solve the following.

1. $3 + 2 \times 4 =$

2. $8 + 6 \times 2 =$

3. $7 + 5 - 8 =$

4. $4 + 10 \div 2 =$

5. $4^2 + 3^2 =$

6. $9 \div 3 \times 8 =$

7. $5(6 + 2) =$

8. $72 \div 8 \times 7 =$

9. $2 \times 15 \div 3 =$

10. $14 - 56 \div 7 =$

11. $9 - 3 + 6 =$

12. $6 + 3 - 2 =$

13. $32 \div 4 \times 3 =$

14. $2 \times 8 \div 4 =$

15. $12 - 30 \div 6 =$

16. $35 \div 5 - 6 =$

17. $5 \times 2 \times 8 =$

18. $15 - 60 \div 5 =$

19. $9 + 20 \div 5 =$

20. $6 - 40 \div 8 =$

Order of Operations

When solving an equation, be sure to follow the **priority pyramid**.

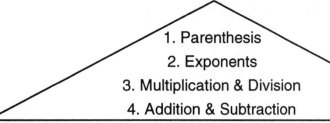

1. Parenthesis
2. Exponents
3. Multiplication & Division
4. Addition & Subtraction

Solve the following.

1. $3 + (6 \times 2) =$

2. $4 + 3(12 - 9) =$

3. $(7 + 2)^2 =$

4. $(9 - 7)^3 - (4 + 3) =$

5. $4(9 - 6)^2 =$

6. $(14 - 6)^2 =$

7. $2(5 + 4) =$

8. $(2 \times 3) + (14 \div 7) =$

9. $7 + 2^2(5 + 2) =$

10. $4 + 7 \times 3 - 8 \times 2 =$

11. $3 + 7^2 =$

12. $(5^2 - 3 \times 5) \div 2 =$

13. $(12 - 8)^3 =$

14. $3 \times 8 - (7 \times 2 + 4) =$

15. $(2^2 + 3)^2 - 4 =$

16. $4^2 - 2^3 =$

17. $5^2 - 4^2 + 2 =$

18. $5 + 3 \times 2 - 4 \div 2 =$

19. $(3^2 + 2 \times 3) \div 5 =$

20. $7^2 - 2(4 \times 3 + 7) =$

Order of Operations

When solving an equation, be sure to follow the **priority pyramid**.

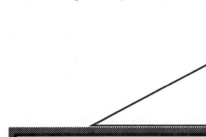

1. Parenthesis
2. Exponents
3. Multiplication & Division
4. Addition & Subtraction

$3 + (3^2 + 9) \div -3 - 1 = 3 + (9 + 9) \div -3 - 1 = 3 + 18 \div -3 - 1 = 3 + -6 - 1 = -4$

Solve the following.

1. $(17 - 9) + 5$

2. $3 \cdot 5 + 9 \cdot 7$

3. $36 \div 9 - 8 + 21 \div 3$

4. $12 \div (3 - 7) + 7$

5. $8 - 4 \cdot 5(2 - 2) + 3$

6. $12 \div (3 + (6 + 3))$

7. $9(3 \div 3) + 4(-5 \cdot 9) \div 3$

8. $5(9 - 8) \cdot 6 + 5 - 3$

9. $3 - (6 \cdot 6) - -3 \cdot 0$

11. $\dfrac{8^2 - 13}{(4 + 9) + 4}$

12. $\dfrac{3^2 - 5 \cdot 7 - 4^2}{(-4 - 9 - 12) + 4}$

13. $\dfrac{(5 - 9)^2 + 2}{(7 - 8)^2 \cdot 3^2}$

14. $\dfrac{5 \cdot 6 - (3 + 4)}{-2^2 - 2^2 + 3^2}$

15. $\dfrac{3^2 - 10}{4^2 - 12}$

16. $\dfrac{3^2 - 1 + 2^2}{3 + 10 - 19 + 32}$

17. $\dfrac{4 + 2 \cdot 3 + 4 - 3}{2^2 \cdot 3^2 - 3}$

18. $3 \cdot (0 - 7) + 8 \div 2^2$

19. $4^2 + 3^2 - 6^2$

Real Number Operations with absolute value

$$-|9 - 12| = -|-3| = -3 \qquad |-5| + |-6| = 5 + 6 = 11$$

The **absolute value** of a number is its distance from zero.
For example: $|5| = 5 \qquad |-6| = 6 \qquad |0| = 0$

Simplify the following.

1. $|-13|$

2. $-|-8|$

3. $|-6| + |8|$

4. $6 + |-4|$

5. $|9| + |-9|$

6. $-|-4 + 7|$

7. $-|-5 + 9|$

8. $|3 - 10|$

9. $-4|4| + |5|$

10. $|4| - |6|$

11. $|23| - |-12|$

12. $|-9| + |13|$

13. $|13| - |-15|$

14. $23 + |8|$

15. $|23| + 9$

16. $|-65| - |-17|$

17. $|4| - |-12| - 4$

18. $7 - |-23| + |-7|$

19. $|1| - |0| + 6$

20. $|-17| - |-17|$

Substitution

Substitute and simplify.

a = 3, b = –9, c = 5

1. $a^2 + b^3 =$

2. $(a + b)^2 =$

3. $a + b - c =$

4. $(c - a)^2 =$

5. $2a - b - 3c =$

6. $(b + c)^2 =$

7. $b^2 + c^2 =$

8. $a^3 - (b + c)^2 =$

9. $-4b + (a + c)^2 =$

10. $abc =$

Substitute and simplify.

a = –6, b = –3, c = 4

1. $3a - 4b =$

2. $7c + b^3 =$

3. $a^2 - b^2 =$

4. $(a - b)^2 =$

5. $a^2 + b^2 =$

6. $(a + b)^2 =$

7. $c^2 - ab =$

8. $2c + 3a - 4b =$

9. $a^2 - (b + c)^3 =$

10. $(a + b + c)^2 =$

Substitution

Substitute and simplify.

x = 2, y = 9, z = –5

1. $x + y + z =$

2. $8x + 3z =$

3. $4y + 3xz =$

4. $xyz \div 10 =$

5. $2(y + z) =$

6. $(y + z)^3 =$

7. $3z + xy =$

8. $(x + y + z)^2 =$

9. $(x + y)^2 =$

10. $(x - z) + y =$

Substitute and simplify.

w = –6, x = 4, y = 3, z = –8

1. $wx + yz =$

2. $2w + 3z - xy + z^3 =$

3. $y(z + x) =$

4. $(w + x + y)^3 =$

5. $(z - w)^3 =$

6. $5(w + x) + 4(y + z) =$

7. $w^2 - x^2 =$

8. $(xy)^2 - 2wz =$

9. $wz - 4xy =$

10. $w + (x + y + z)^2 =$

Combine Like Terms

$$9x + 7y + -21x = -12x + 7y$$

Combine like terms.

1. 5x + 7x

2. 19x + x

3. k – (-8k)

4. -12x +(-4x)

5. 13c – 12c

6. -e + 8e

7. 3yz + 5yz

8. -12n –(-13n)

9. 12b +(-34b)

10. 13ab + (-12ab)

11. 4.7x – 5.9x

12. 7s + 5x –8s

13. 4a + 9 + a

14. 5x – 6y – 8y + 7x

15. 23x + 8 + 6x +3y

16. $4xy + 7xy + 6x^2y + 7xy^2$

17. 2x - y + 2x + 3xy

18. 4x + 3y +(-5y) + 3xy + y

19. 2xy + 7x + 6xy + 3xy +(-3x)

20. $4x^2 +(-7y) +(-4xy) + 9x^2 + 2xy$

Combine Like Terms

$$5(x + 3) + (4x - 7y) + (3x + 2y) = 5x + 15 + 4x - 7y + 3x + 2y = 12x + 15 - 5y$$

Combine like terms.

1. $-2x + 3y - 5x - -8y + 9y$

2. $3x + (-3y) - (5x) + y$

3. $7 - 4y + x + 9y$

4. $-21x + (-2x)$

5. $7(x - y) - 5(2x + 4y)$

6. $-n + 9n + 3 - 8 - 8n$

7. $4(x + 5y) + 3(x + 6y) + 6(3x + 8y)$

8. $12x + 6x + 9x - 3y + -7y + y$

9. $-2(c - d) + (c - d) - 6(c - d)$

10. $-3(4x + -2y) - 2(x + 3y) - 2(2x + 6y)$

11. $3(-4x + 7y) - 3x(2 + 3y)$

12. $2y + 3(2y + 8x) - 3(8y + 2x)$

13. $5(3x^2 - 2y^2) + 3x(x + 3y^2)$

14. $2 \cdot 4x \cdot 3y - 4x \cdot 7y$

15. $3x + 4y + 2x + 5y - 4x$

16. $4(x + 5y) + (5x + y)$

17. $5(x^2 + 3y^2) - y(x^2 + 5y)$

18. $3(2(-y^2 + y) - 3) - 3(2x + y)$

19. $4(x + 9y) - -2(2x + y)$

20. $7x + -2y^2 + 3xy^2 + 2x^2 + 5xy^2$

Solving One-Step Equations (Addition and Subtraction)

$$12 + x = -13$$
$$12 + -12 + x = -13 + -12$$
$$x = -25$$

Solve each equation for the given variable.

1. $y - 12 = 15$

2. $x - 13 = -23$

3. $12 + -g = 14$

4. $3 + x = 9$

5. $-13 + x = 18$

6. $-t + -7 = -56$

7. $27 = v + -5$

8. $-19 + b = 31$

9. $a + 5.7 = 18.9$

10. $-100 = b + -73$

11. $-4 = x - 3$

12. $2\frac{1}{3} + r = 4\frac{2}{9}$

13. $x + 2 = 2(3 - 4)$

14. $-13 = n + (-36)$

15. $c - 3 = 4.7$

16. $r = 4.4 + 3.9$

17. $z + 3.5 = 3.7$

18. $s - 9 = (6 + -8)$

19. $n + \frac{1}{2} = \frac{3}{4}$

20. $12 - -u = 19$

Solving One-Step Equations (Multiplication and Division)

$$5x = 15$$
$$\frac{5x}{5} = \frac{15}{5}$$
$$x = 3$$

$$-\frac{2}{3}y = -8$$
$$-\frac{3}{2} \cdot -\frac{2}{3}y = -8 \cdot \frac{3}{2} \qquad y = 12$$

Solve each equation for the given variable.

1. $6x = -36$

2. $-5x = -20$

3. $-35c = 700$

4. $-12h = 144$

5. $10x = -100$

6. $-30 = 2x$

7. $7x = -84$

8. $4c = 288$

9. $3b = -39$

10. $-(-90) = -45a$

11. $\frac{x}{-8} = \frac{1}{4}$

12. $\frac{4}{x} = \frac{2}{9}$

13. $\frac{-3}{4} = \frac{n}{16}$

14. $\frac{6}{k} = \frac{2}{5}$

15. $-\frac{3}{8} = \frac{x}{24}$

16. $\frac{2}{n} = \frac{1}{9}$

17. $-\frac{x}{6} = \frac{2}{3}$

18. $\frac{x}{6} = \frac{6}{9}$

19. $1.6c = 80$

20. $12.6 = 3b$

Solving Basic Equations

$$4x + 3 = 15$$
$$4x + 3 - 3 = 15 - 3$$
$$4x = 12$$
$$x = 3$$

Solve each equation for the given variable.

1. $4x - 7 = 37$

2. $3x = 6 + -9$

3. $8 - 9y = 35$

4. $7x - 12 = 2$

5. $8 - 12x = 32$

6. $0 = 25x + 75$

7. $4(e + 4) = -12$

8. $3n - 9 = 9$

9. $3(x + 4) + 5 = 35$

10. $9x - 3 = 24$

11. $5 - \frac{1}{2}x = -9$

12. $32 = \frac{4}{6}x - 34$

13. $1.3x + 5 = -5.4$

14. $\frac{x}{3} - 8 = -12$

15. $3 - \frac{1}{5}x = -7$

16. $7 - \frac{1}{9}k = 32$

17. $\frac{2x}{5} + 3 = 9$

18. $4.7 = -3.4m - 5.5$

19. $\frac{3}{12}x + 2 = 11$

20. $8 - \frac{1}{2}y = -6$

Solving Basic Equations

$$9x + 3 = 21$$
$$9x + 3 - 3 = 21 - 3$$
$$9x = 18$$
$$x = 2$$

Solve each equation for the given variable.

1. $5n - 8 = -23$

2. $6x - 2 = 22$

3. $5t - 8 = -18$

4. $6x - 5 = -41$

5. $13x + 7 = -32$

6. $2x + 8 = 6$

7. $-8(r - 2) = 40$

8. $2(w - 6) = 8$

9. $2(f + 7) - 8 = 22$

10. $3x - 4 = -16$

11. $2 + \frac{1}{5}x = -7$

12. $-6 = \frac{3u}{4} + 12$

13. $7.2 + 4x = 19.2$

14. $-3 + 2n = -15$

15. $5 - \frac{1}{2}g = 12$

16. $4k + 7 = -1$

17. $3(c - 2) = 15$

18. $7h + 1 = -13$

19. $5e + -4 = 26$

20. $\frac{m}{3} - 7 = -10$

Solving Basic Equations

$$12x + 3 = 147$$
$$12x + 3 - 3 = 147 - 3$$
$$12x = 144$$
$$x = 12$$

Solve each equation for the given variable.

1. $3(x - 7) = 9$

2. $\dfrac{m}{4} + 6 = 2$

3. $4(c + 2) = -28$

4. $-9r + 5 = -22$

5. $4 + 3g = -14$

6. $7t - 3 + 4t = -25$

7. $14a + 5 - 8a = -1$

8. $2m - 3 - 8m = -27$

9. $-5 + 7d + 3 = 33$

10. $b + 9 - 2b = 6$

11. $4j - 9j + 3 = -32$

12. $3d - 5 - 2d = -9$

13. $2k + 3(k + 4) = -3$

14. $3e + 4e + 1 = 36$

15. $5(j - 4) + j = -8$

16. $12k - 3(k + 5) = 48$

17. $-6r + 12 - 8r = -2$

18. $-j + 3j + 2 = -14$

19. $5(m - 3) + 2m = 27$

20. $4e + 6 - 11e = -8$

Solving Equations with Variables on Both Sides

$$6x - 7 = x + 23$$
$$6x - x - 7 = x - x + 23$$
$$5x - 7 = 23$$
$$5x = 30$$
$$x = 6$$

Solve each equation for the given variable.

1. $2x - 7 = 3x + 4$

2. $-7c + 9 = c + 1$

3. $4(2y - 4) = 5y + 2$

4. $-6 - -2n = 3n - (6 + 5)$

5. $4(t + 5) - 3 = 6t - 13$

6. $2(r - 4) = 5(r + -7)$

7. $7 - 6a = 6 - 7a$

8. $12m - 9 = 4m + 15$

9. $8(x - 3) + 8 = 5x - 22$

10. $3c - 12 = 14 + 5c$

11. $9a + 5 = 3a - 1$

12. $6(x - 9) = 4(x - 5)$

13. $2(x - 4) + 8 = 3x - 8$

14. $3x - 3 = -3x + -3$

15. $-10x + 6 = -7x + -9$

16. $5 + 3x = 7(x + 3)$

17. $\frac{5}{2} x + 3 = \frac{1}{2} x + 15$

18. $2x + 6 = 5x - 9$

19. $4e - 19 = -3(e + 4)$

20. $5t + 7 = 4t - 9$

Problem Solving

| The sum of three times a number and 45 is 67. Find the number. | $3x + 45 = 66$
 $3x + 45 - 45 = 66 - 45$
 $3x = 21$
 $x = 7$ The number is 7. |

Write an equation for each word problem and solve it.

1. The sum of 4 times a number and 5 is –7. Find the number.
   Equation_____

   Solution_____

2. The difference of 5 times a number and 6 is 14. Find the number.
   Equation_____

   Solution_____

3. The product of a number and 5 is 80. Find the number.
   Equation_____

   Solution_____

4. Twice a number added to 7 is 13. Find the number.
   Equation_____

   Solution_____

5. The sum of a number and –6 is 4. Find the number.
   Equation_____

   Solution_____

6. The difference of a number and –3 is 8. Find the number.
   Equation_____

   Solution_____

7. 12 subtracted from 3 times a number is 15. Find the number.
   Equation_____

   Solution_____

8. The quotient of a number and 4 is –8. Find the number.
   Equation_____

   Solution_____

Problem Solving

The sum of three times a number and 45 is 67. Find the number.	$3x + 45 = 66$ $3x + 45 - 45 = 66 - 45$ $3x = 21$ $x = 7$ The number is 7.

Write an equation for each word problem and solve it.

1. The sum of 5 times a number and –11 is –16. Find the number.
   Equation_____

   Solution_____

2. The sum of four times a number and 3 is –13. Find the number.
   Equation_____

   Solution_____

3. 5 times the sum of a number and 2 is 35. Find the number.
   Equation_____

   Solution_____

4. 3 times the sum of a number and negative 2 is –15. Find the number.
   Equation_____

   Solution_____

5. Six times the difference of a number and 9 is 42. Find the number.
   Equation_____

   Solution_____

6. The sum of eight times a number and 3 is 59. Find the number.
   Equation_____

   Solution_____

7. Twelve times the sum of a number and -8 is 36. Find the number.
   Equation_____

   Solution_____

8. The sum of seven times a number and 11 is 81. find the number.
   Equation_____

   Solution_____

Solving Inequalities with Multiple Operations

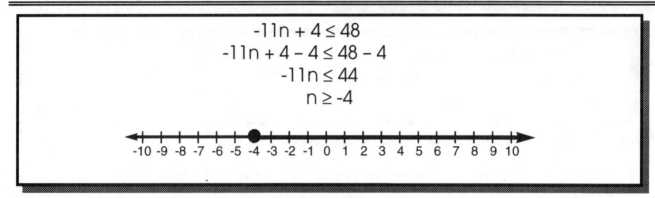

$$-11n + 4 \leq 48$$
$$-11n + 4 - 4 \leq 48 - 4$$
$$-11n \leq 44$$
$$n \geq -4$$

Solve each inequality and graph its solution set.

1. $6x - 3 > 21$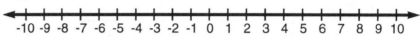

2. $5 > 4x - 7$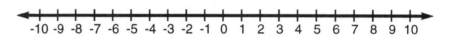

3. $3(3c - 4) \geq 15$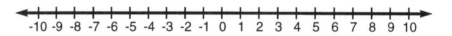

4. $-5x - 10 \geq -10$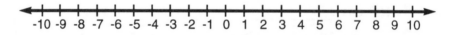

5. $-15 > -3x - 45$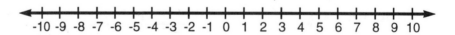

6. $-6(3t + 2) \leq 6$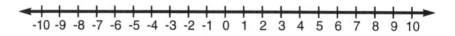

7. $5x - 1 > 9$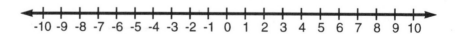

8. $4x - 7 < 9$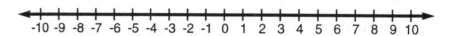

Solving Inequalities with Variables on Both Sides

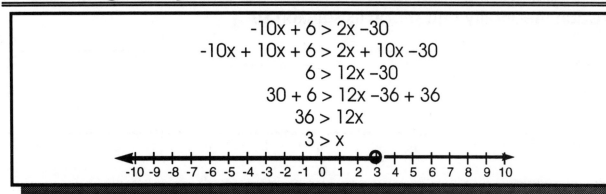

$$-10x + 6 > 2x -30$$
$$-10x + 10x + 6 > 2x + 10x -30$$
$$6 > 12x -30$$
$$30 + 6 > 12x -36 + 36$$
$$36 > 12x$$
$$3 > x$$

Solve each inequality and graph its solution set.

1. $5x + -3 > 2(3 + x)$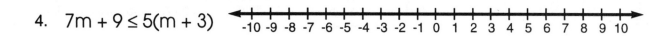

2. $-9 - e > 3e + 11$

3. $3(2x + 4) \geq 7x + 8$

4. $7m + 9 \leq 5(m + 3)$

5. $5x - 20 > 2x + 1$

6. $2(k + 4) \leq 3(2k - 4)$

7. $5c + 2 < 2c + -7$

8. $3(s - 4) \geq 4s - 12$

Practice Solving Inequalities

Solve each inequality and graph its solution set.

1. $12d < d + 11$

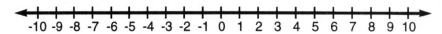

2. $5x \geq -20$

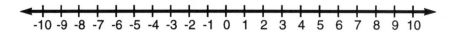

3. $14h \leq 126$

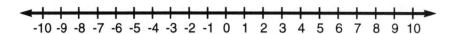

4. $11 \leq 6y - 13$

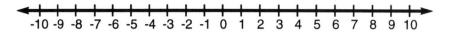

5. $6x - 4 > 2(x - 6)$

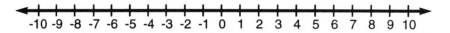

6. $-13t > 52$

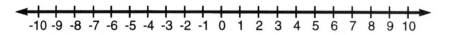

7. $r + 15 \geq 9$

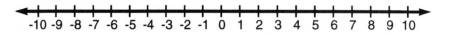

8. $4a - 3 \leq -27$

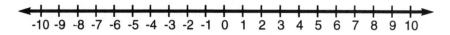

9. $14 + 3x > 6x - 7$

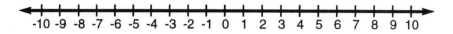

10. $\frac{a}{4} + 3 \leq 5$

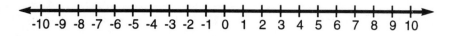

Practice Solving Inequalities

Solve each inequality and graph its solution set.

1. $4w > 2w + 6$

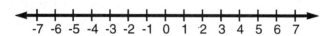

2. $5n + 3 \geq -12$

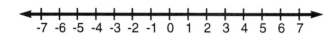

3. $-2a < 5 + 3a$

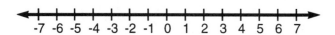

4. $-3.6 > 0.6x$

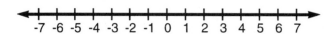

5. $13x \geq -39$

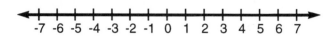

6. $6d < 3d - 18$

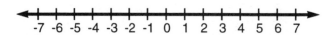

7. $7c - 8 \geq 6$

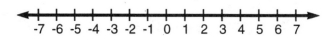

8. $15e - 3 \leq 20e + 12$

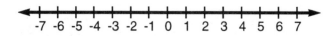

9. $7k < -28$

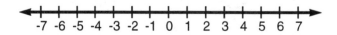

10. $4 + 6r > -8$

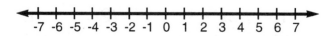

Adding and Subtracting Polynomials

$$(x^2 + 3x + 1) - (3x^2 + 4x - 7) = 4x^2 - x + 8$$

Add or subtract the following polynomials by combining like terms.

1. $(-2x^2 + 4x - 12) + (5x^2 - 5x)$

2. $(3y^2 - 9y) - (-5y^2 + 7y - 7)$

3. $(3x^4 - 2x + 1) - (4x^3 - 5x - 8)$

4. $(6x^3 - 2x^2 - 12) + (6x^2 + 3x + 8)$

5. $(x^2 - x - 4) - (3x^2 - 4x + 5)$

6. $(x^3 - x^2 + 3) - (4x^3 - x^2 + 7)$

7. $(4x^2 + 6x + 3) + (3x^2 - 3x - 2) + (-4x^2 + 3x - 9)$

8. $(7x^2 + 2x + 7) - (4x^2 - 2x + 3) + (-5x^2 + 6x + 7)$

9. $(3x^3 - 5x^2 - 9) - (5x^3 - 5x - 4) - (5x^3 - 4x^2 - 9)$

10. $(2x^2 - 9x - 8) - (2x^3 - 4x^2 + -2)$

11. $(9x^2 - 8x + -4) + (3x^3 - 7x + -5) + (-4x^2 - 2x - 6)$

12. $(3x^2 + 3x + 2) - (5x^3 - 3x^2 + 8) - (-2x^3 + 9x^2 + 8)$

13. $(-2x^3 + 3x^2 + 9) + (-8x^3 - 2x^2 + -4x)$

14. $(-6x^2 - 3x^3 + 4) + (-7x^3 + 2x + 4) - (-3x^3 + 5x^2 + 2)$

15. $(-3x^2 - 4x^3 - 1) - (2x^3 - 7x - 9) - (2x^3 - 2x^2 - 3)$

Raising Exponents to a Power

RULE: $(x^a)^b = x^{ab}$ $(x^2y^3)^3 = x^6y^9$

Multiply the following polynomials.

1. $(xy^3)(x^3y)$

2. $(7xy^3)(-5x^3y^2)$

3. $(x^3y^3)^3$

4. $(-4x^3y^3)^4$

5. $(6x^5y^4)^3$

6. $(x^2y^3)(x^3y^2)$

7. $(-9xy^3)^3$

8. $(-4x^4y^5)^3$

9. $(x^3y)^2$

10. $(3xy^3)^2(-4x^2y^4)^2(2xy^3)$

11. $(-2x^2y^3)^2$

12. $(5x^2y^4)^3$

13. $(-6x^4y^6)^3$

14. $(7xy)^2$

15. $(-3x^3y)^3$

16. $(-2x^2y)^3$

17. $(4x^2y^3)^4$

18. $(2x)^5$

19. $(6x^2y^3)^0$

20. $(-3x^2y)^4$

Multiplying Exponents

Rule: $x^a \cdot x^b = x^{a+b}$ Example: $a^4 \cdot a^3 = a^7$

Multiply the following polynomials.

1. $a \cdot a^2 \cdot a^3 =$

2. $(2a^2b)(4ab^2) =$

3. $(6x^2)(-3x^5) =$

4. $b^3 \cdot b^4 \cdot b^7 \cdot b =$

5. $(3x^3)(3x^4)(-3x^2) =$

6. $(4c^2)(-8c^7) =$

7. $(5xy)(2x^2y^3) =$

8. $(3x)(-4y^2)(6x^3y) =$

9. $(-2c^4)(6cd)(-cd^2) =$

10. $(6k^2)(-3k)(2k^5) =$

11. $(m^2n)(mn^3)(mn) =$

12. $(-4p^3)(-3p^6)(-2p^9) =$

13. $(12e^3)(2g^3)(4eh) =$

14. $(5f)(-3f^3)(2f) =$

15. $(c^2h)(ch^3)(c^3h^4) =$

16. $(3c^2d^2)(-5cd^4) =$

17. $(5x^2y^3)(x^3y)(-x^2y^2) =$

18. $(-4m^3)(-4m^3) =$

19. $d \cdot d^2 \cdot d^3 \cdot d^4 \cdot d^5 =$

20. $(-1)(x)(-x^2)(x)(-x^2) =$

Dividing Exponents

Rule: $\dfrac{x^a}{x^b} = x^{a-b}$	Example: $\dfrac{x^6}{x^4} = x^{6-4} = x^2$	$\dfrac{x^3}{x^{-2}} = x^{3-(-2)} = x^5$

Divide the following polynomials.

1. $\dfrac{x^3}{x}$

2. $\dfrac{9a^3b^5}{-3ab^2}$

3. $\dfrac{d^5}{d^3}$

4. $\dfrac{b^{14}c^9}{b^5c^4}$

5. $\dfrac{-12m^5}{6m}$

6. $\dfrac{15k^7r^3}{-3k^5}$

7. $\dfrac{9a^{13}}{a^3}$

8. $\dfrac{(3xy)\,(4x^2y)}{-6xy^2}$

9. $\dfrac{-14c^{15}d^3}{-2c^9d}$

10. $\dfrac{(5k)\,(-8k^5)}{10k^3}$

11. $\dfrac{18c^3}{-3c^2}$

12. $\dfrac{-48c^2d^4}{-8cd}$

13. $\dfrac{22y^5z^8}{2yz^7}$

14. $\dfrac{28x^2y}{-4x^2}$

15. $\dfrac{-3p^8}{6p^2}$

16. $\dfrac{42r^{13}}{-7r^8}$

17. $\dfrac{(6x^3)\,(4x^9)}{-12x^{10}}$

18. $\dfrac{21k^9}{(3k)\,(7k^4)}$

19. $\dfrac{4x^2y^3z^4}{2xy^2z^3}$

20. $\dfrac{(121c^3)\,(-c^8)}{11c^5}$

Negative Exponents

Rule: $x^{-a} = \dfrac{1}{x^a}$ **Example**: $3^{-2} = \dfrac{1}{9}$ $8x^{-2} = \dfrac{8}{x^2}$ $(4x)^{-3} = \dfrac{1}{64x^3}$

Simplify the following.

1. a^{-6}

2. 2^{-4}

3. b^{-5}

4. $\left(\dfrac{2}{3}\right)^{-1}$

5. c^{-7}

6. $(xy)^{-1}$

7. $\left(\dfrac{3}{4}\right)^{-2}$

8. $(2x)^{-3}$

9. $(c^2d)^{-2}$

10. $(6y^2)^{-2}$

11. $7x^{-3}$

12. m^2n^{-2}

13. $3a^2b^{-3}$

14. $-2x^{-3}$

15. $(-11x^3y)^{-2}$

16. $(-3)^{-3}$

17. $5cd^{-9}$

18. $(-3x^3)^{-2}$

19. $12x^{-8}y$

20. $\left(\dfrac{x^2}{y^3}\right)^{-2}$

Products of Polynomials

$$2y(y - 5) = 2y^2 - 10y$$

Use the distributive property to multiply these polynomials.

1. $3x(x - 3)$

2. $2xy(2x - 3y)$

3. $4a(2a + 4)$

4. $-5y^2(7y - 8y^2)$

5. $-5ab(6a - 4b)$

6. $a(x + 1)$

7. $y(y - 4)$

8. $5b(3 - b)$

9. $4x(x - 3)$

10. $4x^2(3x^2 - x)$

11. $-3x^2(4x^2 - 3x + 3)$

12. $5b(4b^3 - 6b^2 - 6)$

13. $x(x^2 + x + x)$

14. $(3x^4 - 5x^2 - 4)(-3x^3)$

15. $3y (y^2 - 3y + 2)$

16. $-4x^2(5 - 3x + 3x^2 + 4x^3)$

17. $3b(4b^3 - 12b^2 - 7)$

18. $-4x^2(3x^3 + 8x^2 + -9x)$

19. $(-9x^3)(3x^2 - 1)$

20. $(3x^2 - 6x)(-x)$

Products of Polynomials

$(x - 2)(x^2 - x + 4) = x(x^2 - x + 4) - 2(x^2 - x + 4) = x^3 - x^2 + 4x - 2x^2 + 2x - 8$
$$= x^3 - 3x^2 + 6x - 8$$

Use the distributive property to multiply these polynomials.

1. $(5x + 3)(x + 6)$

2. $(4x + y)(3x - 2y)$

3. $(4a + 1)(4a + 1)$

4. $(x + 4)(x + 4)$

5. $(x + y)(3x + y)$

6. $(x + 1)(1 + x)$

7. $(2b - 8)(3b - 7)$

8. $(3x + y)(x^2 + 3x + 4y)$

9. $(4x^2 - 4y^2)(4x^2 + 4y^2)$

10. $(3x^2 - x)(3x - x^2)$

11. $-3x^2(4x^2 - 3x + 3)$

12. $5b(4b^3 - 6b^2 - 6)$

13. $x^2(x^3 + x^2 + x)$

14. $(3x^4 - 5x^2 - 4)(-3x^3)$

15. $(x - y)(x^2 + y^2)$

16. $(4x + 3)(2x - 4)$

17. $(3b - 2)(3b^3 + 6b^2 + 2)$

18. $(3x - 3)(x - 9)$

19. $(-2x^3 + 4)(2x^2 + 5)$

20. $(x - 7)(x + 6)$

Multiplying Binomials

Rule: $(a + b)(a - b) = a^2 - b^2$
Example: $(x - 2)(x + 2) = x^2 + 2x - 2x - 4 = x^2 - 4$

Use the FOIL method or DOTS rule to multiply the following binomials.

1. $(b - 7)(b + 7)$

2. $(5x + y)(5x - y)$

3. $(4a - b)(4a + b)$

4. $(x + 3)(x - 3)$

5. $(c + d)(c - d)$

6. $(x + 1)(x - 1)$

7. $(3b + 7)(3b - 7)$

8. $(3x + y)(3x - y)$

9. $(2x^2 - y^2)(2x^2 + y^2)$

10. $(3x^2 - x)(3x^2 + x)$

11. $(8x^2 - 12)(8x^2 + 12)$

12. $(2b^2 - 2)(2b^2 + 2)$

13. $(3x + 2)(3x - 2)$

14. $(12 + b)(12 - b)$

15. $(x - y)(x + y)$

16. $(x - yz)(x + yz)$

17. $(12b - 4)(12b + 4)$

18. $(7x - 3y)(7x + 3y)$

19. $(-5x^3 + 3)(-5x^3 - 3)$

20. $(x^2 - 8x)(x^2 + 8x)$

Squaring Binomials

Rules: $(a + b)^2 = a^2 + 2ab + b^2$
$(a - b)^2 = a^2 - 2ab + b^2$

Use the FOIL method or Squares of Binomial Formula to multiply the following binomials.

1. $(b + 7a)^2$

2. $(2x + 3v)^2$

3. $(3a - 7b)^2$

4. $(-6x + 3y)^2$

5. $(5c + 9d)^2$

6. $(x - 4y)^2$

7. $(2b - 2c)^2$

8. $(5x + y)^2$

9. $(3x^2 - 3y^2)^2$

10. $(4m^2 - 2n)^2$

11. $(5x^2 - 5y)^2$

12. $(7b^2 - 3c)^2$

13. $(2x - 6y)^2$

14. $(6a + b)^2$

15. $(x - 4y)^2$

16. $(7x - 8y)^2$

17. $(2b^2 - 2c^2)^2$

18. $(-4x + 3y)^2$

19. $(2x - 5y)^2$

20. $(x^2 - 7y)^2$

Area and Perimeter

Find the perimeter of each polygon.

1.

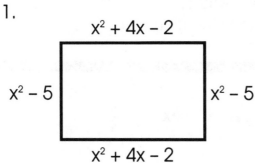

$x^2 + 4x - 2$

$x^2 - 5$ $x^2 - 5$

$x^2 + 4x - 2$

2.

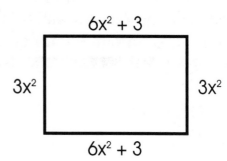

$6x^2 + 3$

$3x^2$ $3x^2$

$6x^2 + 3$

3.

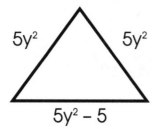

$5y^2$ $5y^2$

$5y^2 - 5$

4.

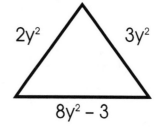

$2y^2$ $3y^2$

$8y^2 - 3$

Find the area of each polygon.

Traingle
Area: $A = \frac{1}{2} bh$

Rectangle
Area: $A = LW$

Square
Area: $A = s^2$

1.

$4x$

$4x$ $4x$

$4x$

2.

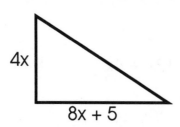

$4x$

$8x + 5$

3.

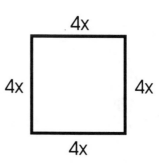

$x^2 + 4x - 2$

$2x$

Factoring Monomials From Polynomials

To **factor a polynomial**, write the polynomial as a product of other polynomials.
For example, $4x^2 - 8x$ can be written as $4x(x - 8)$.
$4x$ is the **Greatest Common Factor (GCF)** of $4x^2$ and $8x$.
$4x$ is a **Common Monomial Factor** of the terms of the binomial.
$x - 8$ is a **Binomial Factor** of $4x^2 - 8$.

Factor.

1. $9a^2 - 18a$

2. $16a^5b^3 + 32a^4b$

3. $x^2 + x^4 + x^3$

4. $3x^5 + 4x^4 - 5x^2$

5. $2x^3 - x$

6. $3a^5 - a^3$

7. $32b^2 + 16b$

8. $5x^3 - 7x^2$

9. $3x^2 - 10x^3$

10. $a^{5n} + a^{3n}$

11. $x^3 - 5x^2$

12. $9c - 3c^2$

13. $5x^4 - 12x^2$

14. $x^2 + x$

15. $6x^2 - 12x^3 - 18x^4$

16. $x^3y^4 + x^2y^2$

17. $18b - 9b^2$

18. $2x^3 + 6x^2$

19. $12x^3 + 4x^2$

20. $x^5 + 3x^2$

Factoring Trinomials of the form x² + bx + c

$$a^2 - 8a + 15 = (a - 5)(a - 3)$$

Factor.

1. $x^2 - 8x + 16$

2. $x^2 - 12x + 20$

3. $x^2 - 12x + 11$

4. $c^2 + c - 20$

5. $x^2 + 12x + 36$

6. $x^2 - x - 6$

7. $x^2 + 12x + 35$

8. $x^2 - 9x + 18$

9. $y^2 - 13y + 42$

10. $x^2 + 6x - 40$

11. $x^2 + x - 132$

12. $x^2 - 8xy + 33y^2$

13. $a^2 - 10ab - 24b^2$

14. $m^2 - 3mn + 2n^2$

15. $x^2 + 15xy + 44y^2$

16. $t^2 + 23t + 42$

17. $y^2 - 12y + 36$

18. $b^2 - 4b - 45$

19. $n^2 + 3n - 18$

20. $c^2 - 10c + 21$

Factoring Trinomials of the form $x^2 + bx + c$

$$x^2 + 3x - 28 = (x + 7)(x - 4)$$

Factor.

1. $x^2 + 4x - 5$

2. $x^2 + 15x + 50$

3. $x^2 + 4x - 32$

4. $x^2 + 7x + 6$

5. $x^2 + 12x + 11$

6. $x^2 + 12x + 20$

7. $x^2 + 2x - 35$

8. $x^2 - 18x + 72$

9. $x^2 - 15x + 56$

10. $x^2 - 6x - 16$

11. $x^2 - 8x + 15$

12. $x^2 + x - 72$

13. $x^2 - 16x + 39$

14. $x^2 + 22x + 121$

15. $x^2 + 13x + 12$

16. $x^2 - 3xy + 2y^2$

17. $x^2 - 14xy + 24y^2$

18. $x^2 + 5xy + 6y^2$

19. $x^2 + 2xy - 63y^2$

20. $x^2 + 8xy - 33y^2$

Factoring Trinomials of the form ax² + bx + c

$$3x^2 - 9x - 12 = 3(x^2 - 3x - 4) = 3(x - 4)(x + 1)$$

Factor.

1. $5x^2 - 10x - 15$

2. $6x^2 - 15x - 21$

3. $3x^2 - 10x + 7$

4. $2x^2 - 11x - 21$

5. $4x^2 + 2x - 20$

6. $3x^2 - 5x - 12$

7. $7x^2 - 26x - 8$

8. $12x^2 - 6x - 18$

9. $6x^2 - 13x + 6$

10. $2x^2 + 9x + 10$

11. $3x^2 - 4x - 32$

12. $4x^2 - 16x + 15$

13. $4x^2 + 7x - 15$

14. $6a^2 - 21a + 15$

15. $11x^2 + 122x + 11$

16. $3x^2 - 20x - 7$

17. $2y^2 - 17y + 35$

18. $4x^2 - 16x + 15$

19. $6x^2 + 25x + 25$

20. $7c^2 - 16c + 9$

Factoring Trinomials of the form ax² + bx + c

$$3x^2 - 9x - 12 = (3x + 3)(x - 4)$$

Factor.

1. $7x^2 + 17x + 6$

2. $5x^2 - 18x + 16$

3. $12x^2 - 40x + 25$

4. $6x^2 - 21x - 12$

5. $4x^2 + 7x - 15$

6. $11x^2 - 122x + 11$

7. $9x^2 - 9x - 28$

8. $2x^2 + 13x + 6$

9. $6x^2 + 5x - 6$

10. $2x^2 - 11x - 40$

11. $10x^2 - 28x - 6$

12. $4x^2 - x - 5$

13. $12x^2 + 16x - 3$

14. $2x^2 + 17x + 35$

15. $15x^2 - 29x - 14$

16. $4x^2 - 7x - 15$

17. $14x^2 - 11x + 2$

18. $2x^2 + 7x + 3$

19. $4x^2 - 15x + 9$

20. $6x^2 + x - 12$

Factoring Trinomials That are Quadratic in Form

$$x^4 - x^2 - 12 = (x^2)^2 - (x^2) - 12 = (x^2 - 4)(x^2 + 3) = (x + 2)(x - 2)(x^2 + 3) = (x^2 - 4)(x^2 + 3)$$

Factor.

1. $x^2y^2 - 8xy + 15$

2. $x^2y^2 - 18xy + 32$

3. $x^2y^2 + 10xy + 24$

4. $x^4 - 8x^2 + 15$

5. $y^4 - 4y^2 - 12$

6. $x^4y^4 - 19x^2y^2 + 34$

7. $2x^2 - 13x + 15$

8. $3x^4 + 20x^2 + 33$

9. $2x^2 - 5x - 12$

10. $8x^4 - 23x^2 - 3$

11. $y^4 + 6y^2 - 16$

12. $x^4y^4 - 8x^2y^2 + 12$

13. $6x^2y^2 - 29xy + 23$

14. $7x^4 + 17x^2 + 6$

15. $x^4y^4 - x^2y^2 - 12$

16. $2x^4y^4 - 7x^2y^2 - 30$

17. $6a^6 + 25a^3b^3 - 25$

18. $4x^4y^4 - 2x^2y^2 - 56$

19. $2x^4 + 13x^2 - 15$

20. $2x^4 + 16x^2 + 30$

Factoring: Difference of Two Squares

Rule: $a2 - b2 = (a + b)(a - b)$ **Example**: $x^2 - 36 = (x + 6)(x - 6)$

Factor.

1. $x^2 - 16$

2. $y^2 - 49$

3. $4x^2 - 1$

4. $81x^2 - 4$

5. $16x^2 - 121$

6. $49x^2 - 36$

7. $1 - 9x^2$

8. $16 - 81x^2$

9. $x^2y^2 - 100$

10. $x^2y^2 - 25$

11. $x^2 - 4$

12. $25 - x^2y^2$

13. $64 - x^2y^2$

14. $4x^2 - y^2$

15. $49x^2 - 16y^4$

16. $a^2 - 1$

17. $c^2 - 16$

18. $a^2 - 36$

19. $b^2 - 9$

20. $y^2 - 81$

Factoring Perfect Square Trinomials

Rule: $a^2 + 2ab + b^2 = (a + b)^2$ $a^2 - 2ab + b^2 = (a - b)^2$
Example: $4x^2 + 4x + 1 = (2x + 1)^2$ $x^2 - 4x + 4 = (x + 2)^2$

Factor.

1. $x^2 - 14x + 49$

2. $b^2 - 18b + 81$

3. $x^2 - 12x + 36$

4. $c^2 - 6c + 9$

5. $x^2 - 2x + 1$

6. $x^2 + 14x + 49$

7. $16x^2 - 40x + 25$

8. $49x^2 + 28x + 4$

9. $4x^2 + 4x + 1$

10. $9x^2 + 12x + 4$

11. $x^2 + 8x + 16$

12. $x^2 - 10x + 25$

13. $a^2 + 12ab + 36b^2$

14. $x^2 - 14x + 49$

15. $9x^2 - 6x + 1$

16. $x^2 - 16x + 64$

17. $y^2 - 24y + 144$

18. $25a^2 - 40ab + 16b^2$

19. $x^2 - 4x + 4$

20. $c^2 - 20c + 100$

Factoring the Sum or the Difference of Two Cubes

Rule:	$x^3 + y^3 = (x + y)(x^2 - xy + y^2)$	$x^3 - y^3 = (x - y)(x^2 + xy + y^2)$
Example:	$x^3 + 8 = (x + 2)(x^2 - 2x + 4)$	$x^3 - 8 = (x - 2)(x^2 + 2x + 4)$

Factor.

1. $x^3 - 1000$

2. $8x^3 - 1$

3. $x^3 - y^3$

4. $x^3 + y^3$

5. $64x^3 + 1$

6. $27x^3 - 8y^3$

7. $x^3y^3 + 64$

8. $x^3 + 125$

9. $64x^3 + 27$

10. $x^3 - 8y^3$

11. $27x^3 + y^3$

12. $1 - 125y^3$

13. $64x^3 + 27y^3$

14. $8x^3 + 27$

15. $64x^3 - y^3$

16. $x^3 - 27$

17. $8x^3 - 216$

18. $125a^3 - 8b^3$

19. $27x^3 - 64$

20. $27x^3 - 1$

Solving Equations by Factoring

The **Multiplication Property of Zero**: The product of a number and zero is zero. The **Principle of Zero Products** states that if the product of two factors is zero, then at least one of the factors must be zero. This principle is used in solving equations.

Solve: $(x - 5)(x - 6) = 0$ If $(x - 5)(x - 6) = 0$, then $(x - 5) = 0$ or $(x - 6) = 0$.

$x - 5 = 0 \quad x - 6 = 0$

$x = 5 \qquad x = 6$

The solutions are 5 and 6.

$$\frac{(x - 5)(x - 6) = 0}{(5 - 5)(5 - 6)} \Big| 0$$
$$0(-1) \Big| 0$$
$$0 = 0$$

$$\frac{(x - 5)(x - 6) = 0}{(6 - 5)(6 - 6)} \Big| 0$$
$$0(-1) \Big| 0$$
$$0 = 0$$

1. $(y + 5)(y + 6) = 0$

2. $x(x + 7) = 0$

3. $(2x + 4)(x + 7) = 0$

4. $(y - 4)(y - 8) = 0$

5. $z^2 - 4 = 0$

6. $(4y - 1)(y + 2) = 0$

7. $y(y - 12) = 0$

8. $4y(3y - 2) = 0$

9. $b^2 - 49 = 0$

10. $m^2 - 100 = 0$

11. $2x^2 - 6x = x - 3$

12. $z^2 - 1 = 0$

13. $(2y - 1)(y - 2) = 0$

14. $x^2 - 5x + 6 = 0$

15. $8t^2 - 32 = 0$

16. $x^2 - x - 2 = 0$

17. $10x^2 - 10x = 0$

18. $x^2 - 3x - 28 = 0$

Problem Solving

The length of a rectangle is 5 in. longer than the width. The area of the rectangle is 50 in.² Find the length and width of the rectangle.
Width of rectangle: w
Length of rectangle: w + 5

A = LW
50 = (w + 5)(w)   Since the width cannot be a negative
50 = w² + 5w   number the answer is 5.
0 = w² + 5w – 50   w + 5 = 5 + 5 = 10
0 = (w + 10)(w – 5)   The length is 10 and the width is 5.
w + 10 = 0   w – 5 = 0

For each word problem, write an equation and solve it.

1. The sum of a number and its square is 30. Find the numbers.

   Equation_____

   Solution_____

2. The sum of twice a number and its square is 143. Find the numbers.

   Equation_____

   Solution_____

3. The sum of a number and its square is 20. Find the numbers.

   Equation_____

   Solution_____

4. For what numbers is the sum of a number and its square equal to 42?

   Equation_____

   Solution_____

5. The square of a number is 70 more than 3 times the number. Find the numbers.

   Equation_____

   Solution_____

6. The square of a number is 35 more than twice the number. Find the numbers.

   Equation_____

   Solution_____

7. The sum of a number and its square is 72. Find the numbers.

   Equation_____

   Solution_____

Problem Solving

The length of a rectangle is 5 in. longer than the width. The area of the rectangle is 50 in.² Find the length and width of the rectangle.

Width of rectangle: w

Length of rectangle: w + 5

$A = LW$

$50 = (w + 5)(w)$ Since the width cannot be a negative

$50 = w^2 + 5w$ number the answer is 5.

$0 = w^2 + 5w - 50$ $w + 5 = 5 + 5 = 10$

$0 = (w + 10)(w - 5)$ The length is 10 and the width is 5.

$w + 10 = 0$ $w - 5 = 0$

For each word problem, write an equation and solve it.

1. The area of a rectangle is 72 m². Its length is twice its width. Find the length and width of the rectangle.

    Equation_____

    Solution_____

2. The width of a rectangle is three more than twice its length. The area of the rectangle is 44in². Find the dimensions of the rectangle

    Equation_____

    Solution_____

3. The area of a square is 144m². Find the length of the sides of the square.

    Equation_____

    Solution_____

4. The area of a rectangle is 27cm². Its width is three times its length. Find the length and width of the rectangle.

    Equation_____

    Solution_____

5. the length of a rectangle is 4 more than twice its width. The area of the rectangle is 96ft². Find its dimensions.

    Equation_____

    Solution_____

Dividing Monomials

$$\frac{25x^9y^6}{5x^7y^8} = \frac{25}{5} \cdot x^{9-7} \; y^{6-8} = \frac{5x^2}{y^2}$$

Simplify.

1. $\dfrac{x^3}{x^5}$

2. $\dfrac{a^4b^2}{2a^2}$

3. $\dfrac{12x^2 \, y^4}{3x^2y^3}$

4. $\dfrac{10a^6b^8}{40a^2b^2}$

5. $\dfrac{14c^2d^2}{28cd}$

6. $\dfrac{18a^9b^3}{36a^2b^2}$

7. $\dfrac{13m^6n^7}{26m^2n^5}$

8. $\dfrac{35x^9y^{10}z^5}{15x^9y^8z^3}$

9. $\dfrac{5x^3y^2z^2}{5x^2yz}$

10. $\dfrac{72x^5y^5z^6}{9x^4yz^3}$

11. $\dfrac{6x^6y^3z^4}{12x^3y^2z^3}$

12. $\dfrac{9x^8y^7z^8}{27x^5y^5z^4}$

13. $\dfrac{18a^6b^2c^6}{36a^4bc^2}$

14. $\dfrac{33x^7y^2}{11x^7yz}$

Simplifying Rational Expressions

$$\frac{a^2+7a+5}{a}=\frac{a^2}{a}+\frac{7a}{a}+\frac{5}{a}$$

$$=a+7+\frac{5}{a}$$

Simplify.

1. $\dfrac{x^3+2x}{x}$

2. $\dfrac{18x+36}{9}$

3. $\dfrac{8y^2+12y^3}{6y}$

4. $\dfrac{10a^6b^8+8a^3b^5}{ab}$

5. $\dfrac{3cd^2+6c^2d}{3cd}$

6. $\dfrac{18x^3-9x^2-3x}{-3}$

7. $\dfrac{m^6n^7+m-n}{m^2n}$

8. $\dfrac{12a^3-9a^2-3a}{-3a}$

9. $\dfrac{9x^4-3x^5-12xy^3}{3xy^3}$

10. $\dfrac{2x^3y^2-2x^3y3^2-4xy^3}{2x^2y^3}$

11. $\dfrac{12a^2-2a+12}{2a}$

12. $\dfrac{9x^8+3x+3}{3x}$

13. $\dfrac{x^3y^3+x-y}{x^3y}$

14. $\dfrac{3x^4y^5+12x^2y^3-18x^2}{x^2y}$

Dividing Polynomials

Simplify: $(x^2 + 6x + 5) \div (x + 1)$

$$\frac{(x^2 + 6x + 5)}{(x + 1)}$$

$$
\begin{array}{r}
x + 5 \\
x + 1 \overline{)x^2 + 6x + 5} \\
\underline{x^2 + 1x} \\
5x + 5 \\
\underline{5x + 5} \\
0
\end{array}
$$

Divide by using long division.

1. $(x^2 + 2x - 35) \div (x + 7)$

2. $(x^2 - 10x + 24) \div (x - 4)$

3. $(x^2 + 4x + 3) \div (x + 1)$

4. $(x^2 + 5x + 6) \div (x + 3)$

5. $(x^2 + 7x + 10) \div (x + 2)$

6. $(x^2 + 4x - 21) \div (x - 3)$

7. $(x^2 + 9x + 8) \div (x + 8)$

8. $(x^2 - 6x + 9) \div (x - 3)$

9. $(x^2 - x - 42) \div (x + 6)$

10. $(x^2 - 3x - 40) \div (x + 5)$

Dividing Polynomials

Simplify: $\dfrac{(4x^2 + 4x - 3)}{(2x + 3)}$

$$
\begin{array}{r}
2x - 1 \\
2x + 3\overline{\smash{)}\,4x^2 + 4x - 3} \\
\underline{4x^2 + 6x} \phantom{{}-3} \\
-2x - 3 \\
\underline{-2x - 3} \\
0
\end{array}
$$

Divide by using long division.

1. $\dfrac{x^2 - 9x + 8}{x - 1}$

2. $\dfrac{2x^2 - 7x - 15}{x - 5}$

3. $\dfrac{4x^2 - 11x - 3}{4x + 1}$

4. $\dfrac{21x^2 + 22x - 8}{3x + 4}$

5. $\dfrac{2x^2 - x - 10}{x + 2}$

6. $\dfrac{x^2 - 4x - 45}{x + 5}$

7. $\dfrac{2x^2 - 5x - 3}{x - 3}$

8. $\dfrac{5x^2 + 43x - 18}{x + 9}$

9. $\dfrac{3x^2 - 27}{x + 3}$

10. $\dfrac{9x^2 - 25x - 6}{x - 3}$

Dividing Polynomials by Synthetic Division

Simplify: $(2x^3 + 3x^2 - 4x + 8) \div (x + 3)$

$$-3 \underline{\big|\ \begin{array}{cccc} 2 & 3 & -4 & 8 \\ & -6 & 9 & -15 \end{array}}$$
$$\begin{array}{cccc} 2 & -3 & 5 & -7 \end{array}$$

$$= 2x^2 - 3x + 5 - \frac{7}{x + 3}$$

Divide by using synthetic division.

1. $(2x^2 + 6x - 8) \div (x + 1)$

2. $(3x^2 + 19x + 20) \div (x + 5)$

3. $(4x^2 + 23x + 28) \div (x + 4)$

4. $(3x^2 - 5) \div (x - 1)$

5. $(3x^2 - 75) \div (x - 5)$

6. $(x^3 - 4x^2 - 36x - 16) \div (x + 4)$

7. $(4x^2 + 9x + 5) \div (x + 1)$

8. $(x^2 + x - 2) \div (x + 2)$

9. $(3x^3 - 13x^2 - 13x + 15) \div (x - 5)$

10. $(2x^3 - 12x^2 + 5x - 30) \div (x - 6)$

11. $(3x^3 + 8x^2 + 9x + 10) \div (x + 2)$

12. $(x^2 + 14x + 45) \div (x + 5)$

13. $(5x^2 - 12x - 9) \div (x - 3)$

14. $(3x^2 - 7x + 6) \div (x - 3)$

Multiplying Rational Expressions

$$\frac{5(x^2 - 25)}{10x^2 + 50x} = \frac{5(x+5)(x-5)}{10x(x+5)} = \frac{x-5}{2x}$$

Simplify.

1. $\dfrac{27x^2 - 75}{4x^2 + 2x} \cdot \dfrac{20x^2 + 10x}{3x + 5}$

2. $\dfrac{14x^2y^4}{24ab^3} \cdot \dfrac{28a^2b^3}{35xy^4}$

3. $\dfrac{x + 4}{6x^3 - 24x} \cdot \dfrac{2x^3 - 8x}{x^2 + 4x}$

4. $\dfrac{x^2 + 5x + 6}{x^2 - 4} \cdot \dfrac{x - 2}{x + 3}$

5. $\dfrac{x^2 + x - 6}{x + 1} \cdot \dfrac{x + 1}{x^2 - 9}$

6. $\dfrac{x^2 + 5x + 4}{x^2 - 16} \cdot \dfrac{3x - 12}{4x + 4}$

7. $\dfrac{x + 2}{x - 3} \cdot \dfrac{x^2 - 8x + 15}{5x - 25}$

8. $\dfrac{x^2 - 1}{x^2 - 2x - 3} \cdot \dfrac{x + 4}{6x - 6}$

9. $\dfrac{12x^2y^4}{36ab^3} \cdot \dfrac{6a^2b^3}{48xy^4}$

10. $\dfrac{x^2 - 12x + 35}{x^2 - 5x - 14} \cdot \dfrac{x^2 + 7x + 10}{x^2 - 25}$

11. $\dfrac{x^2 - 100}{x - 5} \cdot \dfrac{x + 5}{x^2 - 5x - 50}$

12. $\dfrac{4x - 4}{x^2 - 9} \cdot \dfrac{x + 3}{1 - x}$

13. $\dfrac{x^2 + 3x + 2}{x + 7} \cdot \dfrac{x^2 + 9x + 14}{x^2 + 4x + 4}$

14. $\dfrac{2x^2 - 8}{2x + 6} \cdot \dfrac{x^2 - 9}{x^2 - x - 6}$

Dividing Rational Expressions

$$\frac{12x^2y - 4xy}{35z} \div \frac{4x^2y^2 - 8x^2y}{7z^2} = \frac{12x^2y - 4xy}{35z} \cdot \frac{7z^2}{4x^2y^2 - 8xy} = $$

$$\frac{12x^2y^2(x - 2)}{5z^2} \cdot \frac{3z^4}{4x^3y(x - 2)} = \frac{4xy(3x - 1)}{35z} \cdot \frac{7z^2}{4xy(xy - 2)} = \frac{z(3x - 1)}{5(xy - 2)}$$

Simplify.

1. $\dfrac{x + 2}{x + 3} \div \dfrac{x^2 - 4}{x - 2}$

2. $\dfrac{2x^2 + 15 + 18}{x^2 + 5x - 6} \div \dfrac{4x + 6}{x - 1}$

3. $\dfrac{9x^2 + 6x}{x^2 + 6x} \div \dfrac{x^2 - 4}{2x - 4}$

4. $\dfrac{x^2 - x - 12}{x^2 + 11x + 24} \div \dfrac{x^2 - 2x - 8}{x^2 + 8x}$

5. $\dfrac{2x^2 + 6x}{x^2 + 2x} \div \dfrac{x^2 - 9}{4x - 12}$

6. $\dfrac{x^2 - 7x}{x^2 - 14x + 49} \div \dfrac{2x^2 + 6x}{x^2 + x - 56}$

7. $\dfrac{x^2 + 8x}{x^2 + 14x + 48} \div \dfrac{x^2 + x}{x^2 + 7x + 6}$

8. $\dfrac{x + 2}{4x(x - 6)} \div \dfrac{x - 2}{3x(x - 6)}$

9. $\dfrac{25a^4b^2}{8a^2b} \div \dfrac{5ab^3}{6a^3b}$

10. $\dfrac{7 - x}{x + 2} \div \dfrac{x^2 - 49}{x^2 + 9x + 14}$

11. $\dfrac{7x^3y^2}{5xy} \div \dfrac{14x^2y}{10y^2}$

12. $\dfrac{x^2 - 4}{4x + 4} \div \dfrac{x - 2}{x + 1}$

13. $\dfrac{x^2 + 7x + 10}{x^2 + 5x - 14} \div \dfrac{3x + 15}{2x - 4}$

14. $\dfrac{x^2 - 16}{x^2 + 7x + 12} \div \dfrac{5x - 20}{x + 3}$

Adding and Subtracting Rational Expressions

$$\frac{7x-12}{2x^2+5x-12} - \frac{3x-6}{2x^2+5x-12} = \frac{(7x-12)-(3x-6)}{2x^2+5x-12} = \frac{7x-12-3x+6}{2x^2+5x-12} =$$

$$\frac{2(2x-3)}{(2x-3)(x+4)} = \frac{2(2x-3)}{(2x-3)(x+4)} = \frac{2}{x+4}$$

Simplify.

1. $\dfrac{3}{4xy} + \dfrac{6}{3xy} - \dfrac{9}{2xy}$

2. $-\dfrac{8}{4x^2} + \dfrac{6}{4x^2} + \dfrac{9}{4x^2}$

3. $-\dfrac{4x}{x^2+3x-2} + \dfrac{4x}{x^2+3x-2}$

4. $\dfrac{x}{2x-5} + \dfrac{3}{2x-5}$

5. $\dfrac{x}{x-4} + \dfrac{4}{x^2-x-12}$

6. $\dfrac{6a}{a-4} + \dfrac{5}{a+4}$

7. $\dfrac{5}{2xy} + \dfrac{5}{4xy} - \dfrac{12}{6xy}$

8. $-\dfrac{6}{2x^2} + \dfrac{5}{2x^2} + \dfrac{8}{3x^2}$

9. $\dfrac{8x}{x^2-6x-7} + \dfrac{9x}{x^2+9x+8}$

10. $\dfrac{4}{3x-8} - \dfrac{x}{4x-7}$

11. $\dfrac{2}{x+2} + \dfrac{5x}{x^2-4}$

12. $\dfrac{3x}{x^2+4x+4} + \dfrac{6x}{x^2-4}$

Solving Fractional Equations

$$\frac{3}{6} + \frac{8x}{12} = \frac{5}{2} \longrightarrow \text{Multiply both sides of equation by LCD to eliminate all denominators.}$$

$$12\left(\frac{3}{6} + \frac{8x}{12}\right) = 12\left(\frac{5}{2}\right) \longrightarrow \frac{36}{6} + \frac{96x}{12} = \frac{60}{2}$$

$$6 + 8x = 30 \longrightarrow 6 - 6 + 8x = 30 - 6 \longrightarrow 8x = 24 \longrightarrow x = 3$$

Solve.

1. $\dfrac{x}{2} + \dfrac{5}{6} = \dfrac{x}{3}$

2. $\dfrac{6}{x} - \dfrac{2}{8} = \dfrac{x}{8}$

3. $\dfrac{8}{2x-4} = \dfrac{2}{x}$

4. $1 - \dfrac{4}{y} = 5$

5. $5 - \dfrac{3}{x} = 8$

6. $\dfrac{x-2}{10} = \dfrac{1}{5}$

7. $\dfrac{x-5}{x-1} = \dfrac{1}{5}$

8. $\dfrac{3}{4} = \dfrac{x+2}{x-8}$

9. $\dfrac{x-2}{x+6} = \dfrac{1}{9}$

10. $\dfrac{2}{17} = \dfrac{x-6}{x+9}$

11. $\dfrac{x+7}{x-9} = \dfrac{28}{12}$

12. $\dfrac{x+1}{x+5} = \dfrac{5}{9}$

13. $\dfrac{6}{x+4} = \dfrac{x-3}{22-x}$

14. $\dfrac{x+2}{x+7} = \dfrac{7}{12}$

Proportions

Solve.

1. $\frac{x}{30} = \frac{3}{10}$

2. $\frac{5}{15} = \frac{x}{9}$

3. $\frac{x}{15} = \frac{5}{75}$

4. $\frac{2}{x} = \frac{6}{30}$

5. $\frac{5 + x}{10} = \frac{5}{2}$

6. $\frac{x - 1}{10} = \frac{2}{5}$

7. $\frac{x}{20} = \frac{2}{10}$

8. $\frac{x}{5} = \frac{12}{6}$

9. $\frac{x - 2}{8} = \frac{x}{4}$

10. $\frac{x}{6} = \frac{x - 3}{12}$

11. $\frac{x}{3} = \frac{6}{9}$

12. $\frac{x + 1}{7} = \frac{6}{14}$

13. $\frac{6}{x + 5} = \frac{18}{24}$

14. $\frac{4}{x - 3} = \frac{28}{49}$

Problem Solving With Proportions

Four liters of soda cost $4.00. At this rate, how much would 10 liters of soda cost? *To find the cost, write and solve a ratio using x to represent the cost.*

$$\frac{\text{liters}}{\text{cost}} \longrightarrow \frac{4}{4.00} = \frac{10}{x} \longrightarrow 4x = 10(4.00) \longrightarrow 4x = 40 \longrightarrow \frac{4x}{4} = \frac{40}{4}$$

$$x = 10 \longrightarrow \text{The cost of 10 liters of soda is } \$10.00$$

Solve.

1. One hundred thirty-six tiles are required to tile a 30-ft^2 area. At this rate, how many tiles are required to tile a 180-ft^2 area?

2. A stock investment of $4000 earns $320 each year. At the same rate, how much money can a person earn if he invests $6000.00

3. Two gallons of fruit juice will serve 35 people. How much fruit juice is necessary to serve 105 people?

4. A copy machine can print 120 pages per minute. At this rate, how many minutes are required to make 780 copies?

5. The real estate tax for a house that cost $56,000 is $1300. At this rate, what is the value of a house for which the real estate tax is $1700?

Problem Solving With Proportions

Two gallons of gasoline cost $2.00. At this rate, how much would 4 gallons of gasoline cost? *To find the cost, write and solve a proprotion using* x *to represent the cost.*

$\dfrac{\text{gallons}}{\text{cost}} \longrightarrow \dfrac{2}{\$2} = \dfrac{4}{x} \longrightarrow 2x = 8 \longrightarrow \dfrac{2x}{2} = \dfrac{8}{2} \longrightarrow x = 4$

The cost of 4 gallons of gasoline is $4.00

Solve.

1. An aerobics instructor burns 400 calories in 1 hour. How many hours would the instructor have to do aerobics to burn 560 calories?

2. A real estate investment of $37,000 earns $770 each year. At the same rate, how much money must be invested to earn $1,058 each year?

3. Six gallons of paint will cover 120 doors. At this rate, how many gallons of paint are needed to cover 230 doors?

4. A lawnmower can cut 1 acre on a half-gallon of gasoline. At this rate, how much gasoline is needed to cut 3.5 acres?

5. The sales tax on a $15,000 car is $450. At this rate, what is the tax on a $28,000 car?

Graphing Ordered Pairs

(x,y) = (1, -2) Over 1 and down 2
(x,y) = (-3, 4) Over 3 and up 4
(x,y) = (2, -2) Over 2 and down 2

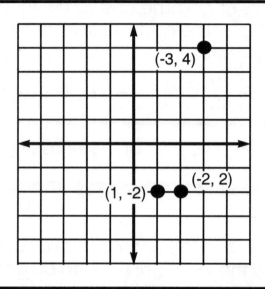

Label the following points.

A (2, -6)
B (1, -3)
C (5, 1)
D (9, 0)
E (5, 3)
F (8, 2)
G (6, 5)
H (7, 1)
I (4, 3)
J (2, 3)
K (6, 3)
L (3, 4)
M (1, 4)

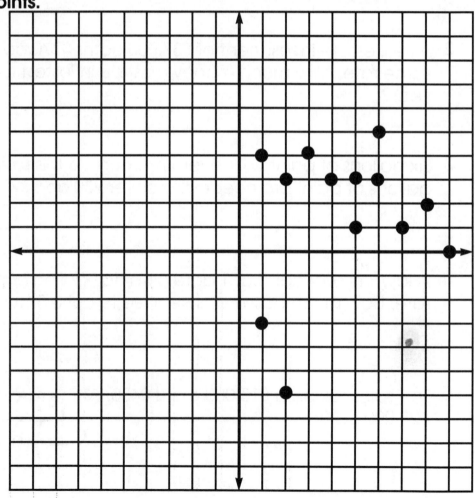

Graphing Ordered Pairs

(x,y) = (1, -2) Over 1 and down 2
(x,y) = (-3, 4) Over 3 and up 4
(x,y) = (2, -2) Over 2 and down 2

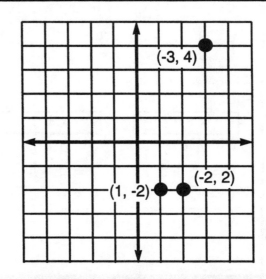

Label the following points.

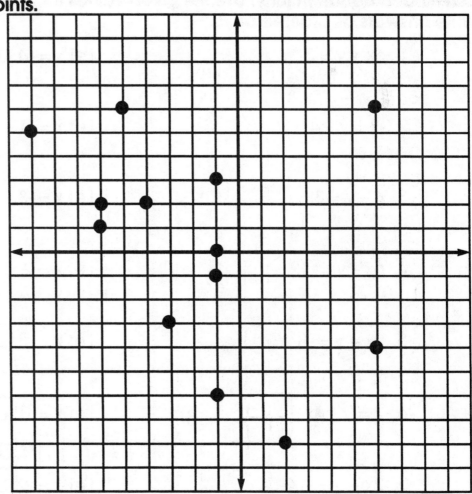

A   (-1, -6)

B   (-3, -3)

C   (-6, 1)

D   (-4, 2)

E   (-6, 2)

F   (-5, 6)

G   (-1, 3)

H   (2, -8)

I   (6, -4)

J   (-9, 5)

K   (-1, -1)

L   (-1, 0)

M   (6, 6)

Plotting Points

$$y - 3 = 4x \qquad \text{Let } x = -2, 1, 2$$
$$y - 3 + 3 = 4x + 3 \qquad \text{Solve for } y$$
$$y = 4x + 3$$

x = -2	x = 1	x = 2
$y = 4 \cdot -2 + 3$	$y = 4 \cdot 1 + 3$	$y = 4 \cdot 2 + 3$
$y = -8 + 3$	$y = 4 + 3$	$y = 8 + 3$
$y = -5$	$y = 7$	$y = 11$
(-2, -5)	(1, 7)	(2, 11)

Solve each equation for y. Use the given values for x to find the values for y. Write answers as ordered pairs.

1. $6x + y = 3$ Let $x = -4, 0, 2$

2. $-x = y - 4$ Let $x = -1, -2, -3$

3. $4 - y = 3x$ Let $x = -3, 1, -2$

4. $6x - y = -12$ Let $x = 2, 3, -2$

5. $2x + y = -8$ Let $x = -3, 2, 4$

6. $2 = y - 4x$ Let $x = -1, 0, 2$

7. $2x + y = -14$ Let $x = -2, 0, 3$

Graphing Ordered Pairs

Solve for y in each equation. Choose 3 values for x and find the values for y.
Graph the 3 ordered pairs and draw a line connecting them.

$$y - 3 = 2x$$
$$y - 3 + 3 = 2x + 3$$
$$y = 2x + 3$$

x	y
-2	-1
0	3
1	5

$$y = 2 \cdot -2 + 3$$
$$y = -4 + 3$$
$$y = -1$$

$$y = 2 \cdot 0 + 3$$
$$y = 0 + 3$$
$$y = 3$$

$$y = 2 \cdot 1 + 3$$
$$y = 2 + 3$$
$$y = 5$$

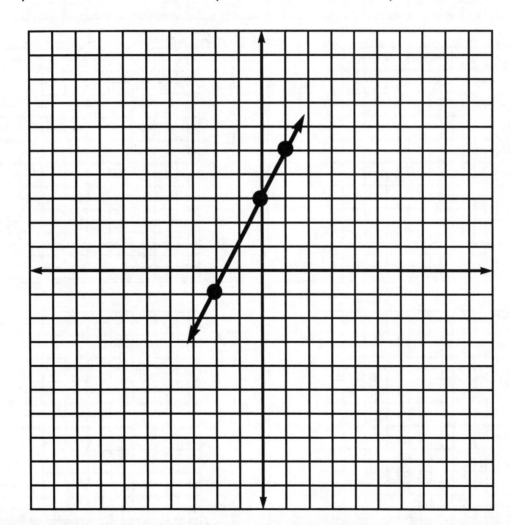

Graphing Linear Equations

Graph each equation by plotting points.

1. $y = x + 4$

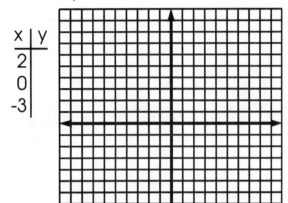

x	y
2	
0	
-3	

2. $y = 2x - 7$

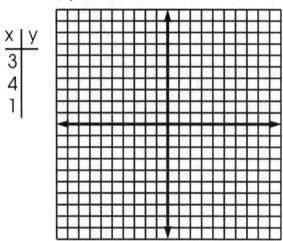

x	y
3	
4	
1	

3. $4x + y = 8$

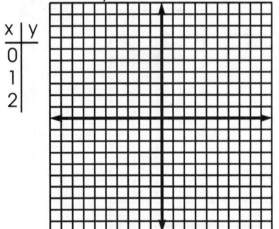

x	y
0	
1	
2	

4. $2x + 6y = 12$

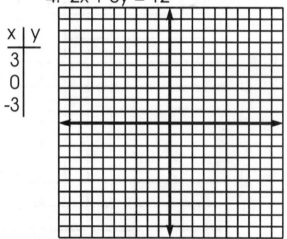

x	y
3	
0	
-3	

5. $x + y = 5$

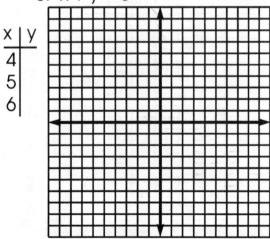

x	y
4	
5	
6	

6. $y = 6 - x$

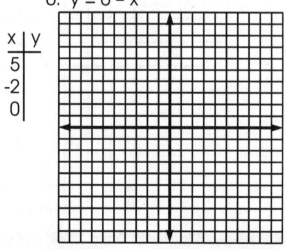

x	y
5	
-2	
0	

Graphing Linear Equations

Graph each equation by plotting points.

1. $y = x + 2$

x	y
-3	
2	
-2	

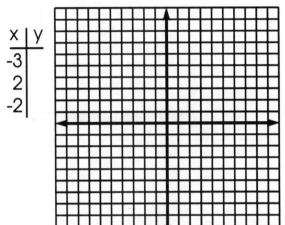

2. $y = 4x - 9$

x	y
4	
2	
0	

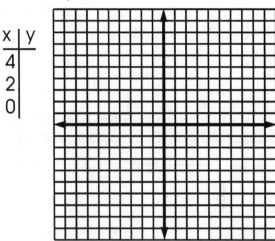

3. $2x + 2y = 8$

x	y
3	
-5	
-2	

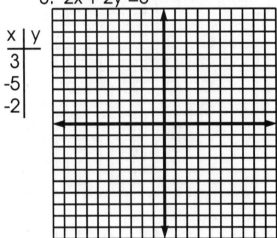

4. $3x + y = 9$

x	y
1	
3	
2	

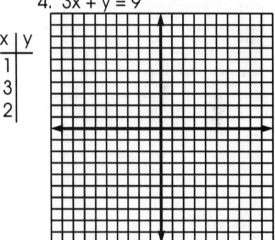

5. $x + y = 6$

x	y
3	
-3	
2	

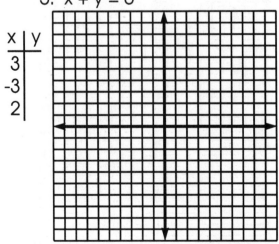

6. $y = 9 - x$

x	y
0	
4	
3	

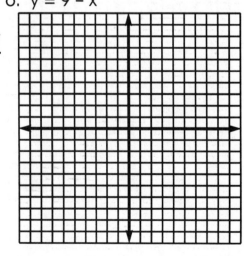

 CD-3732

Slope-Intercept Form

The **slope** of a line containing two points, P_1 and P_2, whose coordinates are (x_1,y_1) and (x_2,y_2), is given by:

Slope = $m = \dfrac{y_2 - y_1}{x_2 - x_1}$, $x_2 \neq x_1$

To find the **y-intercept (b)**, let x = 0.

$8x - 2y = -6$
$y = 4x + 3$
$m = \dfrac{4}{1}$ (up)
     (to right)
$b = 3$

Solve for y, state the m and b, and graph.

1. $5x + y = -10$

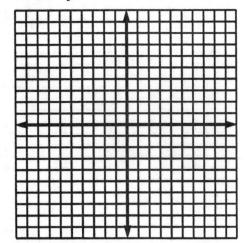

2. $y - 4x = 8$

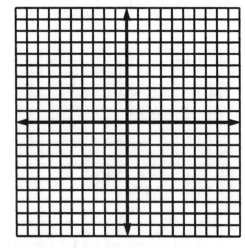

3. $2x + 2y + 4 = 0$

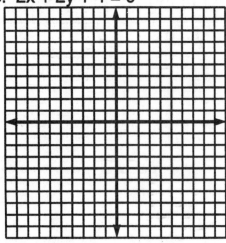

4. $3x - 4y = -12$

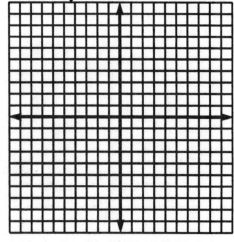

CD-3732

Slope-Intercept Form

Solve for y, state the m and b, and graph.

1. y = 3x − 6

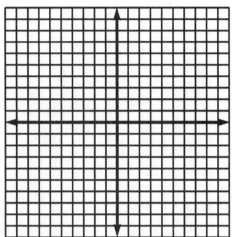

2. 5x − y = 7

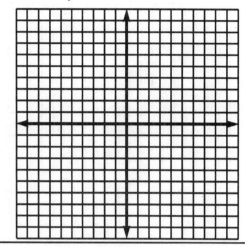

3. 2x + 3y =9

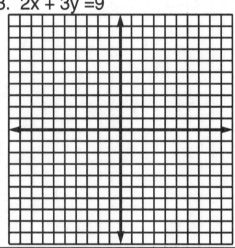

4. x − 3y + 6 = 0

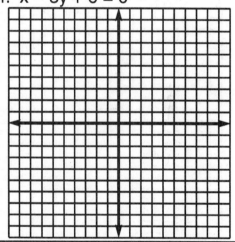

5. 6x + 8y = 12

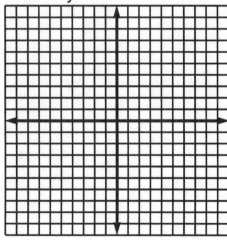

6. x − 4y + 4 = 12

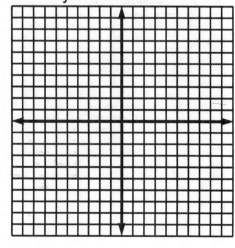

Slope-Intercept Form

Solve for y, state the m and b, and graph.

1. $3y = 4x - 12$

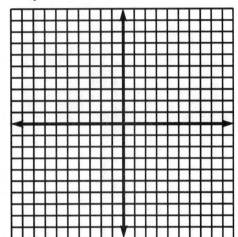

2. $6x - 6y = 12$

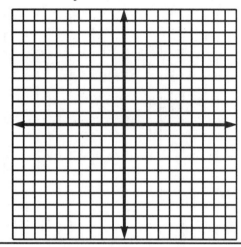

3. $4x + 7y = 14$

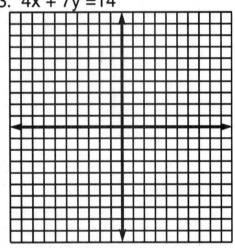

4. $6x - 4y + 4 = 0$

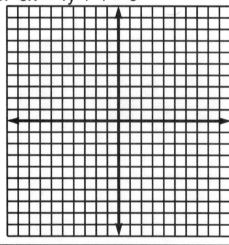

5. $5x + 3y = 18$

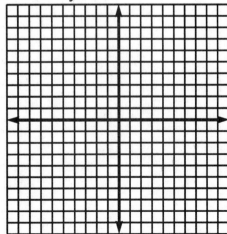

6. $4x - 6y + 8 = 14$

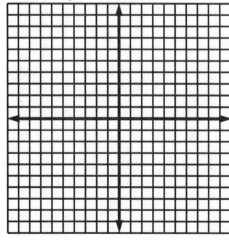

X and Y Intercepts

To find x-intercept, let y = 0. To find y-intercept, let x = 0.
Graph $4x - y = 4$ by using the x- and y-intercepts.

x-intercept	**y-intercept**
$3x - y = 3$	$3x - y = 3$
$3x - 0 = 3$	$3(0) - y = 3$
$3x = 3$	$-y = 3$
$x = 1$	$y = -3$

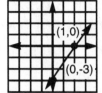

Find the x- and y-intercepts and graph.

1. $x + 5y = 10$

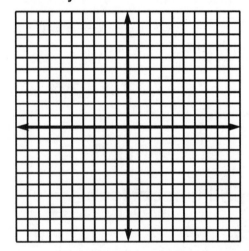

2. $3x - 6y = 12$

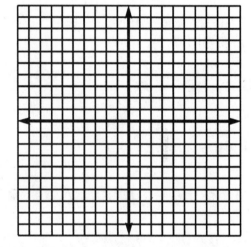

3. $4x + 2y = -8$

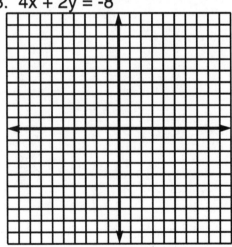

4. $2x + 6y = 18$

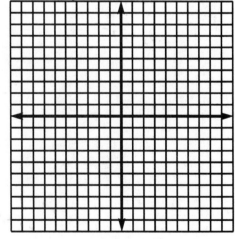

Name_____

Graphing

Writing an Equation of a Line

> **Slope-intercept Form of a Straight Line**
> For all equations of the form y = mx + b, m is the slope of the line.
> The y-intercept is (0,b). This equation, y = mx + b, is
> the **slope-intercept form of a straight line.**
> When the equation is in the form Ax + By = C, solve the equation
> for y. Once you have solved for y, follow the same procedure used
> for an equation in the form y = mx + b.

Write each equation below in slope-intercept form.

1. $2y - x = 6$

2. $3y = 2x + 12$

3. $4y + 24 = 3x$

4. $4y - x = 32$

5. $-4x + y = 8$

6. $y - x + 5 = 0$

7. $-9x + 3y + 27 = 0$

8. $y - 6 = 2x$

Find the equation of a line using the slope-intercept form: y = mx + b.

1. $m = 0 \qquad b = \frac{3}{5}$

2. $m = -5 \qquad b = \frac{3}{4}$

3. $m = \frac{3}{4} \qquad b = \frac{2}{3}$

4. $m = -\frac{9}{5} \qquad b = -3$

5. $m = \frac{1}{4} \qquad b = \frac{1}{3}$

6. $m = \frac{3}{7} \qquad b = \frac{2}{3}$

7. $m = \frac{3}{5} \qquad b = \frac{1}{5}$

Name_____

Writing an Equation of a Line

<table>
<tr><td>

Slope-intercept Formula

y = mx + b

m is slope

b is y intercept containing

coordinate points (x,y)

</td><td>

m = 4 passing through points (1,2)
Using this information, {m=4, x=1, y=2}
Substitute into y = mx + b to find b
2 = (4)(1) + b ⟶ 2 = 4 + b ⟶
⟶ –4 +2 =–4 + 4 + b ⟶ –2 = b with
this information m=4, b=–2, write equation
as y = 4x –2

</td></tr>
</table>

Find the equation of the line with given slope passing through the indicated point P.

1. m = -2, P(4,5)

    b=

    Equation_____

2. m = 2 , P (5,7)

    b=

    Equation_____

3. m = 2, P(–1,–6)

    b=

    Equation_____

4. m = 1 , P (–4,3)

    b=

    Equation_____

5. m = 2, P(–1,1)

    b=

    Equation_____

6. m = 0 , P (3,5)

    b=

    Equation_____

7. m = -5, P(6,–1)

    b=

    Equation_____

8. m = –7 , P (–7,–7)

    b=

    Equation_____

9. m = 5, P(3,5)

    b=

    Equation_____

10. m = 3 , P (–2,–3)

    b=

    Equation_____

11. m = 4, P(2,–6)

    b=

    Equation_____

12. m = –8 , P (2,8)

    b=

    Equation_____

Graphing Linear Inequalities

To Graph: $y > 2x + 3$

1. Graph line $y = 2x + 3$ $m = \dfrac{2}{1}$ $b = 3$

2. If > or <, connect with dotted line   3. If ≥ or ≤, connect with solid line

The coordinate plane is now divided into 2 regions.

4. Test any (x,y) on each side of line which divides plane into the 2 regions. Test (x,y) in original inequality.

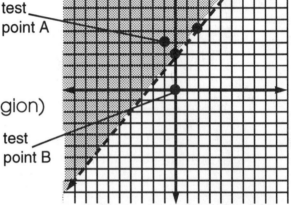

$y > 2x + 3$
Test point A (–1, 4)
Is 4 > 2 (–1) + 3?
4 > –2 + 3
4 > 1 ⟶ true
(Shade this region)

$y > 2x + 3$
Test point b (0,0)
Is 0 > 2 (0) + 3?
0 > 0 + 3
0 > 3 ⟶ false
(Do not shade this region)

test point A

test point B

Graph the solution set.

1. $x + 4y > 8$

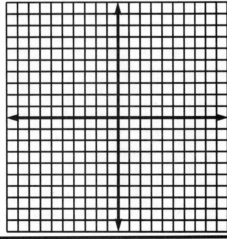

2. $4x + 5y > 10$

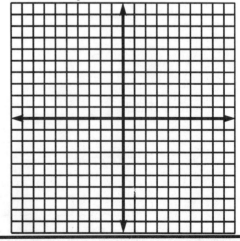

76   CD-3732

Graphing Linear Inequalities

Graph the solution set.

1. $5x - 4y > 10$

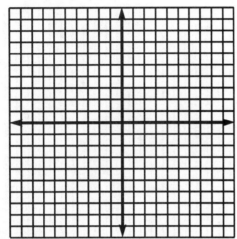

2. $3x + 2y \geq 6$

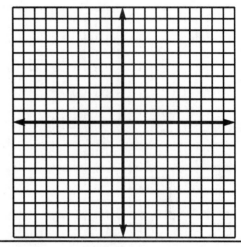

3. $3x + y < 6$

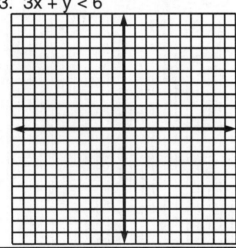

4. $3x - 4y \leq 12$

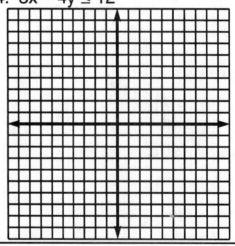

5. $2x + 3y \geq 6$

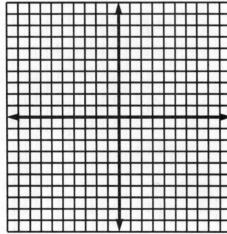

6. $2x + y < 4$

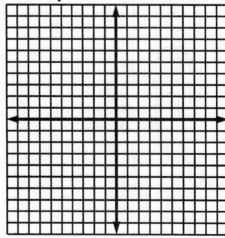

Graphing Linear Inequalities

Graph the solution set.

1. $5x + 5y < 15$

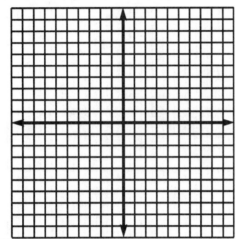

2. $y + 6 > 0$

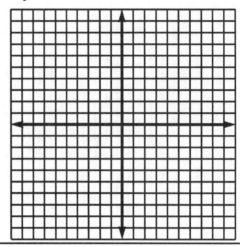

3. $x + 2 < 0$

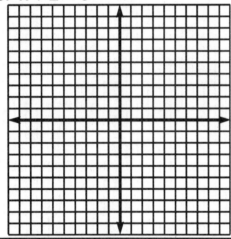

4. $3x - 5y < 10$

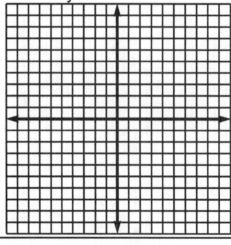

5. $5x - 3y > 15$

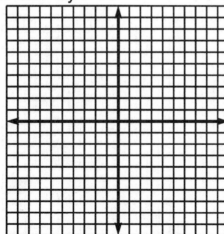

6. $5x - 2y \leq 10$

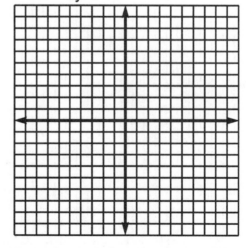

 CD-3732

Solving Systems of Linear Equations by Graphing

Two or more equations considered together is called a **system of equations**. The following example is a system of two linear equations in two variables.

x + 2y = 4
2x + y = −1

The graphs of these equations are straight lines.
An ordered pair that is a solution of each equation of the system is a **solution of the system of equations in two variables**.
The solution of a system of linear equations can be found by graphing the lines of the system. The solution of the system of equations is the point where the lines of the ordered pair intersects.

Solve by graphing:
x + 2y = 4
2x + y = -1
Graph each line and find the point of intersection.

The solution is (-2, 3) because the ordered pair lies on each line.

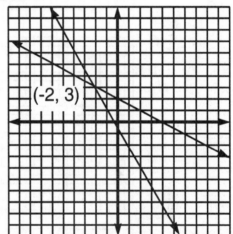

(-2, 3)

Solve by graphing.

1. x + y = 4
    x − y = 2

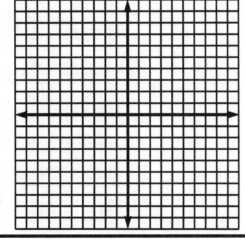

2. x + y = 2
    3x − y = -6

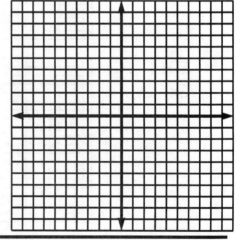

Solving Systems of Linear Equations by Graphing

Solve by graphing.

1. x + y = 3
    x − y = 5

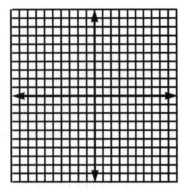

2. x − y = -4
   3x − y = -10

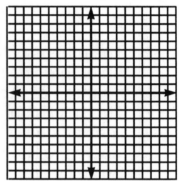

3. x − y = -2
    x + 2y = 10

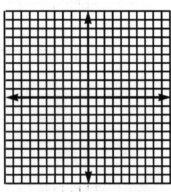

4. 4x − 2y = 8
    y = 3

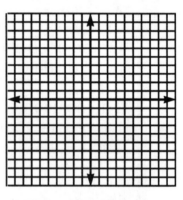

5. x = 5
    y = -1

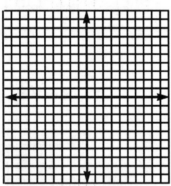

6. 3x − 4y = 12
   5x + 4y = -12

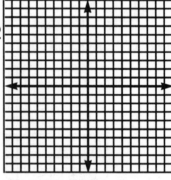

7. x = 4
    3x - 2y = 4

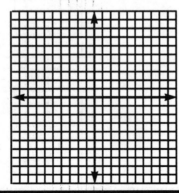

8. y = 2x + 3
    y = x + 6

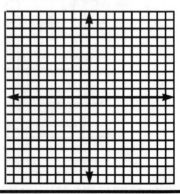

CD-3732

Solving Systems of Linear Equations by Graphing

Solve by graphing.

1. $y = x - 7$
   $x = 2y + 6$

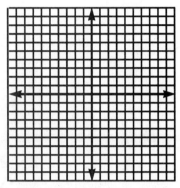

2. $x - 4y = 2$
   $x + 2y = 8$

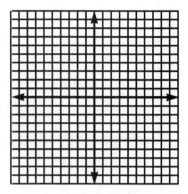

3. $y = 3x + 5$
   $x + y = 1$

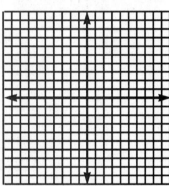

4. $y = x - 3$
   $y + x = 1$

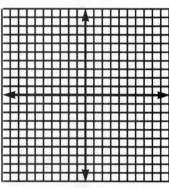

5. $x + y = 6$
   $3x - y = 2$

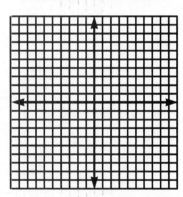

6. $2x + y = 6$
   $3x + y = 12$

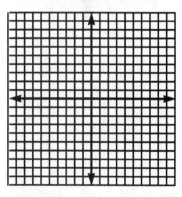

7. $y = x + 3$
   $2y = 3x + 1$

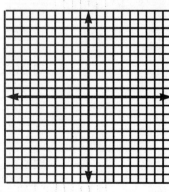

8. $-2x + y = 0$
   $2x + 3y = -8$

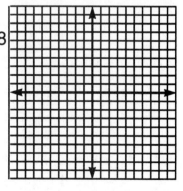

 CD-3732

Solving Systems of Equations by Addition Method

$$2x + 3y = 7$$
$$\underline{x - 3y = -1}$$
$$3x \quad\quad = 6$$
$$\frac{3x}{3} = \frac{6}{3}$$
$$\mathbf{x = 2}$$

Substitute 2 for x in 2x + 3y = 7

$$2x + 3y = 7$$
$$2(2) + 3y = 7$$
$$4 + 3y = 7$$
$$3y = 3$$
$$\mathbf{y = 1}$$

answer (2,1)

1. $3x + y = 5$
   $x - y = 7$

2. $x + 4y = 2$
   $-x + y = 8$

3. $3x - 4y = 14$
   $x + 4y = 2$

4. $2x - 7y = 3$
   $-2x + y = -9$

5. $y = 2x - 3$
   $-y = x$

6. $y = 5x + 1$
   $2y = -5x + 2$

7. $3x + y = 8$
   $x - y = 4$

8. $2x - y = 6$
   $3x + y = 4$

9. $x + y = 7$
   $x - y = 1$

10. $2x - 5 = y$
    $x - 7 = -y$

11. $5x - 3y = -1$
    $4x + 3y = 10$

12. $8x - 3y = 1$
    $-8x + 5y = 9$

13. $3y - 4x = 5$
    $y + 4x = 7$

14. $2x - 2y = 14$
    $x + 2y = 1$

 CD-3732

Solving Systems of Linear Equations by Multiplication with Addition Method

1. solve the following

$6x + 5y = 6$
$6x - 3y = 6$

2. $6x + 5y = 6$
$(-1)(6x - 3y = 6)$ } Multiplication to create additive inverse

3. $6x + 5y = 6$
$\underline{-6x + 3y = -6}$ } Addition method
$8y = 0$
$y = 0$

4. $6x + 5y = 6$ } Substitute
$6x + 5(0) = 6$
$6x = 6$
$x = 1$

Solve the following.

1. $3x + 6y = 6$
   $2x + y = 1$

2. $3x - 4y = 0$
   $x - y = 1$

3. $4x - 4y = 12$
   $3x + 2y = 4$

4. $2x - 3y = 14$
   $x + 3y = 7$

5. $3x + 5y = 16$
   $2x - y = 2$

6. $8x + 3y = -21$
   $4x + 5y = -7$

7. $3x + y = 4$
   $x + 3y = 4$

8. $x + y = -1$
   $2x - y = -5$

9. $3x + y = 8$
   $x + 2y = 1$

10. $x + 5y = -7$
    $2x + 7y = -8$

83

Solving Systems of Linear Equations by Substitution

$$4x + 4y = 12$$
$$3x + y = 9 \longrightarrow y = 9 - 3x$$
$$4x + 4(9 - 3x) = 12$$
$$4x + 36 - 12x = 12$$
$$36 - 8x = 12$$
$$-8x = -24$$
$$x = 3$$

Solution (3,0)

Solve the following.

1. $x + y = 5$
   $x = y + 7$

2. $3x - y = 7$
   $y = x + 3$

3. $2x + 7y = 8$
   $x + 5y = 7$

4. $4x - 7y = 9$
   $y = x - 3$

5. $2x + 4y = 6$
   $2x + y = -3$

6. $x + 3y = 17$
   $2x + 3y = 22$

7. $3x + y = 5$
   $2x + 3y = 8$

8. $x - y = 1$
   $2x + y = 8$

9. $y = 3 - 2x$
   $y = 2 - 3x$

10. $y = 2x + 3$
    $y = 4x + 4$

11. $y = 3x + 3$
    $y = 2x + 4$

12. $2x + 7y = -1$
    $3x + y = 8$

13. $3x + 4y = 26$
    $-2x + y = 1$

14. $2x + 6y = 24$
    $x - 4y = -2$

Simplifying Radicals

$$\sqrt{36x^2y^{12}} = 6\sqrt{x^2y^{12}} = 6xy^6$$

Simplify.

1. $\sqrt{x^{16}}$

2. $\sqrt{x^8}$

3. $\sqrt{x^{14}y^6}$

4. $\sqrt{x^3y^9}$

5. $\sqrt{x^9y^9}$

6. $\sqrt{8x^3}$

7. $\sqrt{25x^8y^2}$

8. $\sqrt{27x^8}$

9. $\sqrt{54x^8}$

10. $\sqrt{a^{14}}$

11. $\sqrt{8x^2}$

12. $\sqrt{81x^6}$

13. $\sqrt{25x^6}$

14. $\sqrt{8x^9}$

15. $\sqrt{64x^9y^{12}}$

16. $\sqrt{9a^4b^8}$

17. $\sqrt{16x^4}$

18. $\sqrt{125b^{15}}$

19. $\sqrt{121y^{12}}$

20. $\sqrt{x^2y^{10}}$

Simplifying Radicals

$$\sqrt{81x^2y^6} = \sqrt{9x^2y^{12}} = 6xy^3$$

Simplify.

1. $\sqrt{4x^4}$

2. $\sqrt{81x^6}$

3. $\sqrt{12x^4y^8}$

4. $\sqrt{9x^3y^4}$

5. $\sqrt{6x^9}$

6. $\sqrt{18x^3y^4}$

7. $\sqrt{4x^5y^2}$

8. $\sqrt{9x^5y^{16}}$

9. $\sqrt{6x^2}$

10. $\sqrt{x^3}$

11. $\sqrt{12x^2y^4}$

12. $\sqrt{121x^6}$

13. $\sqrt{27x^5}$

14. $\sqrt{9x^3}$

15. $\sqrt{16x^5y^4}$

16. $\sqrt{64a^3b^6}$

17. $\sqrt{4x^7}$

18. $\sqrt{21x^2}$

19. $\sqrt{12y^4}$

20. $\sqrt{9x^6}$

Multiplying Radical Expressions

$$\sqrt{2a} \ \sqrt{4a} = \sqrt{8a^2} = \sqrt{2 \cdot 4 \cdot a^2} = 2a\sqrt{2}$$

Simplify.

1. $\sqrt{9} \ \sqrt{32}$

2. $3\sqrt{5} \ 2\sqrt{4}$

3. $4\sqrt{3x} \ 4\sqrt{4x}$

4. $5\sqrt{4a} \ 2\sqrt{6a}$

5. $3\sqrt{8a} \ 8\sqrt{3a}$

6. $6\sqrt{9xy} \ 4\sqrt{2xy}$

7. $2\sqrt{4x^3y} \ 3\sqrt{3a^2b^2}$

8. $4\sqrt{9a^6b} \ 4\sqrt{9a^4b^4}$

9. $2\sqrt{2a^6} \ 5\sqrt{3a^3b^5}$

10. $3\sqrt{4x^3y} \ 4\sqrt{5x^5y^7}$

11. $\sqrt{2x^4} \ \sqrt{10x^2y^2}$

12. $4\sqrt{x^3} \ 3\sqrt{4x}$

13. $\sqrt{xy} \ 2\sqrt{xy}$

14. $x\sqrt{81} \ y\sqrt{36}$

15. $2\sqrt{9x^2} \ 2\sqrt{4x^2}$

16. $x\sqrt{3x} \ x\sqrt{2x^2}$

17. $3\sqrt{2x^3} \ 3\sqrt{3x^2y^2}$

18. $x\sqrt{5x^3y} \ x\sqrt{5x^2y}$

19. $5\sqrt{2x^6y} \ 3\sqrt{3x^3y^5}$

20. $2\sqrt{4x^3y} \ y\sqrt{x^5y^7}$

Dividing Radical Expressions

$$\sqrt{\frac{12}{3}} = \sqrt{4} = 2 \qquad\qquad \sqrt{\frac{4}{25}} = \frac{\sqrt{4}}{\sqrt{25}} = \frac{2}{5}$$

Simplify.

1. $\sqrt{\dfrac{3x^4y^3}{x^2y^2}}$

8. $\sqrt{\dfrac{12x^3}{3x}}$

2. $\sqrt{\dfrac{16x}{9x}}$

9. $\sqrt{\dfrac{8x^3}{2x}}$

3. $\sqrt{\dfrac{12x^2}{48}}$

10. $\sqrt{\dfrac{50x^2}{2}}$

4. $\sqrt{\dfrac{3x^2}{75y^2}}$

11. $\sqrt{\dfrac{36x}{25x^3}}$

5. $\sqrt{\dfrac{x^2}{25}}$

12. $\sqrt{\dfrac{49}{9}}$

6. $\sqrt{\dfrac{9}{64}}$

13. $\sqrt{\dfrac{4x^3y}{4xy^3}}$

7. $\sqrt{\dfrac{27x^2}{3}}$

14. $\sqrt{\dfrac{2x^2}{18x^4}}$

Adding and Subtracting Radical Expressions

$$2\sqrt{y} + 3\sqrt{y} + \sqrt{y} = 6\sqrt{y} \qquad \sqrt{4x} + 3\sqrt{x} = 2\sqrt{x} + 3\sqrt{x} = 5\sqrt{x}$$

Simplify.

1. $4\sqrt{2x^3} + 3\sqrt{2x^3}$

2. $3\sqrt{2y} + 2\sqrt{2y}$

3. $2\sqrt{4x} + 3\sqrt{2x} - 2\sqrt{2x} + 4\sqrt{4x}$

4. $4\sqrt{x} - 2\sqrt{x} - 3\sqrt{x} + 5\sqrt{x}$

5. $3\sqrt{x^3} + 3\sqrt{x^2}$

6. $4\sqrt{y^3} - 2\sqrt{y^3}$

7. $x\sqrt{x^3} + x\sqrt{x^3}$

8. $3y\sqrt{2y} - y\sqrt{2y}$

9. $2\sqrt{50} - 4\sqrt{8} - 3\sqrt{72}$

10. $2\sqrt{5y} + 4\sqrt{5y} + 3\sqrt{5y}$

11. $3\sqrt{6x} + 5\sqrt{6x}$

12. $2\sqrt{y} - 4\sqrt{y}$

13. $x\sqrt{27} + x\sqrt{12}$

14. $3\sqrt{x^3} - 4\sqrt{x^3}$

15. $y\sqrt{y^3} - y\sqrt{y^3}$

16. $x\sqrt{6x} + x\sqrt{24x}$

17. $3\sqrt{9x^2y^2} + 2\sqrt{9x^2y^2}$

18. $3x\sqrt{4x^3y} - 5\sqrt{x^3y}$

19. $5\sqrt{24y} + 3\sqrt{54y}$

20. $3\sqrt{4x^2y} - 8y\sqrt{y}$

Solving Equations by Taking Square Roots

$$x^2 = 36$$
$$\sqrt{x^2} = \sqrt{36}$$
$$x = \pm 6$$

The solutions are 6 and -6

Solve by taking square roots.

1. $x^2 = 9$

2. $x^2 = 144$

3. $x^2 - 49 = 0$

4. $x^2 = 100$

5. $a^2 - 169 = 0$

6. $x^2 - 49 = 0$

7. $a^2 = 196$

8. $x^2 - 25 = 0$

9. $x^2 - 81 = 0$

10. $x^2 - 64 = 0$

11. $3x^2 - 108 = 0$

12. $2a^2 - 32 = 0$

13. $4x^2 - 16 = 0$

14. $2x^2 - 128 = 0$

15. $3x^2 - 432 = 0$

16. $x^2 - 121 = 0$

17. $3x^2 - 27 = 0$

18. $5x^2 - 125 = 0$

19. $x^2 + 81 = 162$

20. $x^2 - 16 = 0$

Solving Quadratic Equations by Factoring

$x^2 - 6x = -9$	$x - 3 = 0$
$x^2 - 6x + 9 = 0$	$x = 3$
$(x - 3)(x - 3) = 0$	The solution is 3

Solve by factoring.

1. $x^2 - 4x = 0$

2. $a^2 - 36 = 0$

3. $y^2 + 9y = 0$

4. $y^2 + 49y = 0$

5. $y^2 + 5y - 6 = 0$

6. $y^2 - y - 6 = 0$

7. $3u^2 - 12u + 9 = 0$

8. $6x^2 + 12x = 0$

9. $x^2 + 7x = 0$

10. $x + 8 = x(x + 3)$

11. $y^2 - 8x + 12 = 0$

12. $a^2 - 7a = -12$

13. $y^2 + 15 = 8y$

14. $2x^2 + x = 6$

15. $5a^2 + 25a = 0$

16. $x^2 - 6x + 5 = 0$

17. $x - 6 = x(x - 4)$

18. $4x^2 + 16x = 0$

19. $3x^2 - 9x = 0$

20. $x - 25 = x(x - 9)$

Solving Quadratic Equations by Factoring

Solve by factoring.

1. $x^2 - 6x + 9 = 0$

2. $x^2 + 7x + 10 = 0$

3. $x^2 = 4x - 4$

4. $3x^2 - 13x + 4 = 0$

5. $6y^2 - 7y + 2 = 0$

6. $x^2 = 10x - 25$

7. $x^2 + 3x - 10 = 0$

8. $r^2 - 15r = 16$

9. $4a^2 + 9a + 2 = 0$

10. $2a^2 + a - 6 = 0$

11. $4a^2 + 15a - 4 = 0$

12. $9x^2 = 18x + 0$

13. $x^2 - 5x + 6 = 0$

14. $2x^2 = 9x + 5$

15. $2x^2 - 9x + 9 = 0$

16. $6x^2 = 23x + 18$

17. $3x^2 - 2x - 8 = 0$

18. $x^2 = 4x + 5$

19. $a^2 - 6a = 0$

20. $x^2 + 3x - 4 = 0$

21. $x^2 + 7x + 12 = 0$

22. $x^2 + 5x - 6 = 0$

Solving Quadratic Equations by Taking Square Roots

$$x^2 = 36$$
$$\sqrt{x^2} = \sqrt{36}$$
$$x = \pm 6$$
The solutions are 6 and -6

Solve by taking square roots.

1. $x^2 = 36$

2. $x^2 = 16$

3. $4x^2 - 81 = 0$

4. $x^2 = 64$

5. $a^2 - 4 = 0$

6. $9a^2 - 16 = 0$

7. $a^2 = 4$

8. $x^2 - 36 = 0$

9. $x^2 - 49 = 0$

10. $x^2 - 16 = 0$

11. $3x^2 - 75 = 0$

12. $3a^2 - 27 = 0$

13. $3(x + 3)^2 = 27$

14. $(x + 2)^2 = 4$

15. $4(x - 3)^2 = 16$

16. $3x^2 - 48 = 0$

17. $6x^2 - 54 = 0$

18. $(x + 1)^2 = 36$

19. $4(x + 2)^2 = 64$

20. $(x + 2)^2 = 36$

Probability Experiment-Directional Page

Directional Page

Review all terms given on these worksheets and follow the directions below. Answer all questions with your partner.

1. Designate one partner "A" and one partner "B".

2. On your worksheet, calculate the theoretical probability for tossing a fair coin and getting "heads" (H) and "tails" (T). Record these probabilities on the worksheet as directed, changing all fractions to decimals for ease of comparison.

3. Answer questions #1, 2, and 3 on your worksheet now!

4. Get one fair coin from your teacher.

5. "A" flips the coin 10 times while "B" records each outcome as "H" for Heads or "T" for tails.

6. For the next 10 coin flips, "B" flips the coin while "A" records the outcomes.

7. Continue alternating tasks every 10 coin tosses until you have completed 100 coin tosses.

8. Analyze this experimental data to the theoretical probability you calculated earlier.

9. Answer questions # 4 and #5 on the worksheets.

10. There should be a grid on the board to hold all of the experimental data from each cooperative group. Partner "A" should then write their group's experimental data on the board. Class discussion of combined data.

11. After the class discussion of the combined data, refine your answer to question # 5 on worksheet . Write at least two sentences comparing class data to your own experimental data.

Extension Activity: Toss the coin 25, 50, or 100 more times and record the results !!!

***Teacher's note- Each group should receive the following:
1 Directional page
1 Terminology and calculations page
1 Tally sheet
1 Question page
1 Fair coin (penny)

Probability Experiment
Terminology and Calculations Page

Probability is the chance that a given event will occur, expressed mathematically as a ratio from 0 (no chance) to 1 (almost certain).

Sample Space is the set of all possible outcomes of an event.

Outcomes represent each member of the sample space.

Theoretical Probability is the ratio of the number of possible outcomes of a given event to the total number of outcomes in the sample space. In other words, theoretical probability is which outcomes will probably occur, given the variables of the situation. We will denote this as P(H) and P(T), for the theoretical probability of "heads" and "tails," respectively.

Sample Space : Fair Coin {   }

Calculate:

P(H) = { no. of times H occurs in sample space } = _____ = 0._____
           total no. of outcomes in sample space

P(T) = { no. of times T occurs in sample space } = _____ = 0._____
           total no. of outcomes in sample space

Experimental Probability is the ratio of the frequency of an event to the number of random experiments conducted. We will denote this as P(H) and P(T), for the theoretical probability of "heads" and "tails," respectively.

Flip a coin 50 times. Record (H) for heads and (T) for tails after each flip. Use your experimental data to calculate:

Sample Space: 10 Flips {   }
25 Flips {   }
50 Flips {   }

P(H)= { No. of heads} = _____ = 0._____   P(T) = { No. of tails} = _____ = 0._____
              10   10   10   10

P(H)= { No. of heads} = _____ = 0._____   P(T) = { No. of tails} = _____ = 0._____
              25   25   25   25

P(H)= { No. of heads} = _____ = 0._____   P(T) = { No. of tails} = _____ = 0._____
              50   50   50   50

Probability Experiment

Questions Page

Names_____

As cooperative pairs, answer the following questions.

1. Of what similarly sounding word does "probability" remind you?

2. Explain in your own words the difference between theoretical and experimental probabilities.

3. What predictions (conjectures) can you make about the results of your experiment based on the theoretical probability of tossing "heads" or "tails"? In other words what do you think will happen when you toss a coin 10, 50 , and 100 times and analyze the results.

4. Analyze the results of your experiment. Does your experimental probability confirm or contradict your original predictions about the likelihood of tossing a fair coin and getting "heads" or "tails"?

5. Make a statement about the relationship between experimental and theoretical probabilities of a given event based on your experiment.

Probability Experiment

Tally sheet

Names_____

Write an H or T next to each number as the coin is flipped. Record the total number of H's or T's per ten coin flips in the end column.

										H	T
Key: H=Heads T=Tails											
1	2	3	4	5	6	7	8	9	10		
11	12	13	14	15	16	17	18	19	20		
21	22	23	24	25	26	27	21	29	30		
31	32	33	34	35	36	37	38	39	40		
41	42	43	44	45	46	47	48	49	50		
51	52	53	54	55	56	57	58	59	60		
61	62	63	64	65	66	67	68	69	70		
71	72	73	74	75	76	77	78	79	80		
81	82	83	84	85	86	87	88	89	90		
91	92	93	94	95	96	97	98	99	100		

 CD-3732

 CD-3732

Reproducible 1/4 inch graph paper

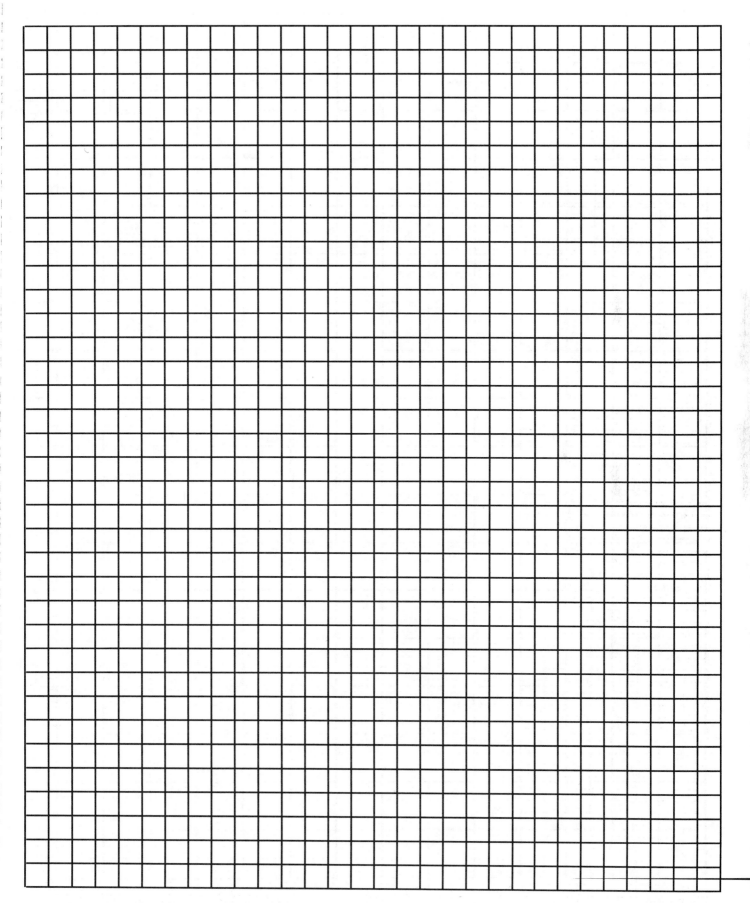

Reproducible 1/2 inch graph paper

100

101 CD-3732

Great Work!

———————————————

receives this award for

———————————————

Keep up the great work!

———————————— ————————————

signed   date

Algebra Superstar

———————————————

is an Algebra Superstar!

———————————————

You are terrific!

———————————— ————————————

signed   date

CD-3732

Algebra Award

_____

receives this award for

_____

Keep up the great work!

_____ _____

signed   date

Algebra Whiz!

_____

receives this award for

_____

Great Job!

Grect Job!

_____ _____

signed   date

CD-3732

Page 1

Operations on the Real Numbers

Integers
The integers are ...,-4, -3, -2, -1, 0, 1, 2, 3, 4, ...
As you can see, there are three dots before and after the list of integers. This means that there is no largest integer or smallest integer.

On a number line, the integers to the right of zero are **positive integers** and the integers to the left of zero are the **negative integers**. Zero is neither a positive integer or a negative integer.

The **natural numbers** are all positive integers.
1, 2, 3, 4, ...
The **whole numbers** consist of all of the positive integers and zero.
0, 1, 2, 3, 4, ...

A **variable** is a letter of the alphabet that is used in mathematics to stand for a number. For example, in the problem 2t = 10, t is the variable.

The quotient of two integers is a **rational number**. A rational number can be written as $\frac{x}{y}$, in the case that x and y are integers and y is not equal to zero (y≠0). A rational number written this way is called a fraction.

Every integer is a rational number. A number written as a decimal, such as 3.5, is also a rational number.

All rational numbers can be written as a repeating or terminating decimal.

An **irrational number** is a number whose decimal expansion does not terminate and never repeats. For example π =3.141592604...

The **rational numbers** and the **irrational numbers** make up the **real numbers**.

Page 2

Patterns

French mathmetician Blaise Pascal developed a triangular pattern to describe the coefficients for the expansion of (a + b), for consecutive values of "n" in rows. In the triangular formation below, note that $(a + b)^0 = 1$ and $(a + b)^1 = a + b$.

Part A. Directions In Pascal's triangle below, fill in the blanks to extend the pattern.

```
n = 0                        1
n = 1                     1     1
n = 2                   1    2    1
n = 3                 1   3    3   1
n = 4               1   4    6    4   1
n = 5             1   5   10  10   5   1
n = 6           1   6   15  20  15   6   1
n = 7         1   7   21  35  35  21   7   1
n = 8       1   8   28  56  70  56  28   8   1
n = 9     1   9   36  84  126 126 84  36   9   1
```

Part B. For the problems below, use Pascal's triangle to find the coefficients of the expansion (a + b).

1. $(a + b)^3 = \underline{1}a^3 + \underline{3}a^2b + \underline{3}ab^2 + \underline{1}b^3$

2. $(a + b)^6 = \underline{1}a^6 + \underline{6}a^5b + \underline{15}a^4b^2 + \underline{20}a^3b^3 + \underline{15}a^2b^4 + \underline{6}ab^5 + \underline{1}b^6$

3. $(a + b)^4 = \underline{1}a^4 + \underline{4}a^3b + \underline{6}a^2b^2 + \underline{4}ab^3 + \underline{1}b^4$

4. $(a + b)^7 = \underline{1}a^7 + \underline{7}a^6b + \underline{21}a^5b^2 + \underline{35}a^4b^3 + \underline{35}a^3b^4 + \underline{21}a^2b^5 + \underline{7}ab^6 + \underline{1}b^7$

Page 3

Patterns

Carefully study the patterns of numbers below. Complete each pattern.

(x10) 1. 10, 100, 1,000, 10,000, **100,000**, **1,000,000**, **10,000,000**

-2,+10 2. 17, 15, 25, 23, 33, 31, **41**, **39**, **49**, **47**

÷10 3. 800, 80, 8, 0.8, 0.08, **0.008**, **0.0008**, **0.00008**, **0.000008**

X2 4. 1, 4, 9, 16, 25, **36**, **49**, **64**, **81**, **100**

+5,-1 5. 1, 6, 5, 10, 9, 14, 13, **18**, **17**, **22**, **21**

$\frac{x}{x+1}$ $\frac{x+1}{x+2}$ 6. $\frac{1}{2}, \frac{2}{3}, \frac{3}{4}, \frac{4}{5}, \frac{5}{6}, \frac{6}{7}$ $\frac{7}{8}$ $\frac{8}{9}$ $\frac{9}{10}$ $\frac{10}{11}$

x³ 7. 7, 21, 63, 189, **567**, **1,701**, **5,103**, **15,309**

-5 8. 125, 120, 115, 110, **105**, **100**, **95**, **90**

mult2,+b. 3, 6, 7, 14, 15, 30, 31, **62**, **63**, **126**, **127**

x10÷5 10. 2, 20, 4, 40, 8, 80, 16, **160**, **32**, **320**, **64**

CHALLENGE! The following is a special pattern called the Fibonacci sequence. See if you can discover and complete this interesting pattern.

1, 1, 2, 3, 5, 8, 13, **21**, **34**, **55**, **89**, **144**

1+1=2,+3...

Page 4

The Addition of Real Numbers

-8 + 5 = -3

Add.

1. 8 + (-7) **1**

2. -55 + -8 + -4 + 54 **-13**

3. -21 + 12 + -1 + -19 **-29**

4. 3 + 12 + -13 + 36 **38**

5. 18 + 21 + (-3) + 9 **45**

6. 9 + 7 + -7 + -9 **0**

7. 12 + 7 + -16 + 9 + -34 **-22**

8. 2.7 + (-4.8) **-2.1**

9. 8.3 + (3.9) **12.2**

10. 5.8 + 8.4 **14.2**

11. $-5\frac{3}{4} + (-2\frac{3}{4}) + 8$ **$-\frac{1}{2}$**

12. $3\frac{5}{8} + (-1\frac{2}{3}) + 2$ **$3\frac{23}{24}$**

13. $3\frac{3}{5} + 4\frac{4}{7}$ **$8\frac{1}{35}$**

14. $-3\frac{1}{6} + (-9\frac{3}{12}) + 6$ **$-6\frac{5}{12}$**

15. 2.76 + -6.56 + -9.72 **-13.52**

16. 3.45 + 2.65 + -9.43 **-3.33**

17. $-2\frac{3}{5} + (-5\frac{3}{7}) + 3$ **$-5\frac{1}{35}$**

18. $-8\frac{3}{5} + 3\frac{3}{7}$ **$-5\frac{6}{35}$**

19. 3.54 + 4.27 + 7.43 **15.24**

20. 7.867 + -5.329 **2.538**

Answer Key

Worksheet 5 — The Addition of Real Numbers

Name_____ *Operations with Real Numbers*

The Addition of Real Numbers

$$-12 + 4 = -8$$

Add.

1. $2 + 5 + -3$ **4**
2. $12 + -9 + 17$ **20**
3. $34 + -13 + -8 + 0 + 34$ **47**
4. $21 + 3 + -9 + 22$ **31**
5. $21 + 9 + (-6) + 7$ **31**
6. $3 + (-3) + 4 + (-5)$ **-1**
7. $2 + -5 + -5 + 2$ **-6**
8. $3.6 + (-2.5) + -5.5$ **-4.4**
9. $(-.6) + -.56 + 3$ **1.84**
10. $2.2 + -3.4 + 5.1$ **3.9**

11. $-6\frac{2}{5} + (-3\frac{2}{5}) + 7$ **$-2\frac{4}{5}$**
12. $2\frac{3}{5} + (-3\frac{2}{5}) + -6$ **$-6\frac{4}{5}$**
13. $2\frac{1}{2} + 6\frac{1}{2}$ **9**
14. $-2\frac{1}{3} + (-5\frac{7}{10}) + -7$ **$-15\frac{1}{30}$**
15. $8.43 + -9.98 + -3.23$ **-4.78**
16. $2.54 + -5.21 + -6.34$ **-9.01**
17. $-1\frac{2}{5} + (-3\frac{2}{3}) + 4$ **$-1\frac{4}{15}$**
18. $-7\frac{3}{4} + 2\frac{3}{4}$ **$-4\frac{3}{4}$**
19. $2.54 + -5.87 + -32.65$ **-35.98**
20. $4.983 + 5.342$ **10.325**

Worksheet 6 — The Subtraction of Real Numbers

Name_____ *Operations with Real Numbers*

The Subtraction of Real Numbers

$$9 - (-2) = 9 + 2 = 11$$

Subtract.

1. $45 - 129$ **-84**
2. $18 - (-13)$ **31**
3. $-201 - (-42)$ **-159**
4. $38 - 39 - (-13)$ **12**
5. $9 - (-2) - 8 - 7$ **-4**
6. $35 - 67 - 85 - 21 - 12$ **-150**
7. $12 - 7 - -16 - 9 - -34$ **46**
8. $0 - 21$ **-21**
9. $9 - (-32)$ **41**
10. $-34 - 6$ **-40**

11. $-\frac{2}{5} - \frac{2}{5} - (-\frac{1}{2})$ **$\frac{-3}{10}$**
12. $-\frac{4}{7} - \frac{1}{7} - (\frac{6}{7})$ **$-1\frac{4}{7}$**
13. $\frac{3}{8} - \frac{5}{8}$ **$-\frac{1}{40}$**
14. $9.432 - 4.348 - 32.938$ **-27.864**
15. $3.9 - 5.9$ **-2**
16. $3.434 - 9.294$ **-5.86**
17. $8 - -(12)$ **20**
18. $9 - 3.8$ **5.2**
19. $2.19 - 7.8 - 8.31$ **-13.92**
20. $-7 - (-2)$ **-5**

Worksheet 7 — The Subtraction of Real Numbers

Name_____ *Operations with Real Numbers*

The Subtraction of Real Numbers

$$8 - (-3) = 8 + 3 = 11$$

Subtract.

1. $232 - 45$ **187**
2. $23 - (-21)$ **44**
3. $321 - (-34)$ **355**
4. $245 - 32 - (-36)$ **249**
5. $8 - (-5) - 7 - 9$ **-3**
6. $43 - 78 - 35 - 21$ **-91**
7. $66 - 35 - 74 - 32$ **75**
8. $-45 - 0$ **-45**
9. $4 - (-8)$ **12**
10. $-19 - 8$ **-27**

11. $-\frac{2}{3} - \frac{1}{3} - (-\frac{1}{3})$ **$\frac{-2}{3}$**
12. $-\frac{2}{5} - \frac{1}{2} - (\frac{2}{5})$ **$-1\frac{7}{10}$**
13. $\frac{2}{5} - \frac{1}{3}$ **$\frac{2}{15}$**
14. $2.456 - 4.345 - 5.457$ **-7.346**
15. $4.3 - 7.6$ **-3.3**
16. $4.346 - .4537$ **3.8923**
17. $7 - (-22)$ **29**
18. $4 - 3.8$ **0.2**
19. $5.34 - 9.9 - 3.65$ **-8.21**
20. $-9 - (-6)$ **-3**

Worksheet 8 — The Multiplication of Real Numbers

Name_____ *Operations with Real Numbers*

The Multiplication of Real Numbers

$$(-3)(-4) = 12$$

Multiply.

1. $-9 \cdot 12$ **-108**
2. $(4)(8)$ **32**
3. $(12)(-3)(4)$ **-144**
4. $(0)(2)(-213)$ **0**
5. $(-5)(-5)(-5)$ **-125**
6. $(-3)(-9)$ **27**
7. $(-3)(0)$ **0**
8. $12(-3)$ **-36**
9. $(7)(-9)(-12)$ **756**
10. $(5)(2)(-1)$ **-10**

11. $(21.2)(-3.95)$ **-83.74**
12. $(7.56)(3.2)(4.3)$ **104.0256**
13. $(2.22)(-1.11)$ **-2.4642**
14. $6(23)$ **138**
15. $(-\frac{2}{3})(-1.6)$ **$1\frac{1}{15}$ or $1.0\overline{6}$**
16. $(-\frac{5}{9})(9.9)$ **$\frac{-55}{10}$ or -5.5**
17. $(-\frac{3}{5})(\frac{3}{5})$ **$\frac{-9}{25}$**
18. $(-\frac{4}{5})(2.2)$ **$\frac{-88}{50}$ or -1.76**
19. $(2.4)(-1.4)$ **-3.36**
20. $-7(-7)$ **49**

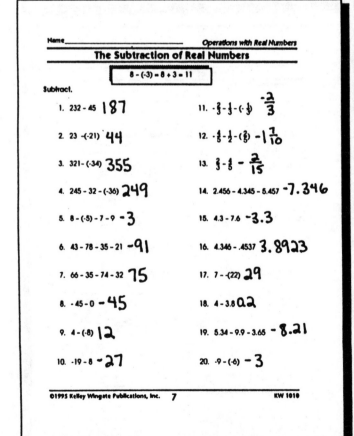

Worksheet 1 (page 9)

Name_____
Operations with Real Numbers

The Division of Real Numbers

$$7 \div 3.5 = 2$$

Divide.

1. $-47 \div 7 = -6\frac{5}{7}$ or $-6.\overline{714285}$
2. $45 \div (-8) = -5\frac{5}{8}$
3. $-36 \div (4) = -9$
4. $65 \div 15 = 4\frac{1}{3}$ or $4.\overline{3}$
5. $0 \div (-8) = 0$
6. $520 \div (0) = $ undefined
7. $\frac{36}{6} = 6$
8. $\frac{105}{5} = 21$
9. $\frac{102}{17} = 6$
10. $\frac{54}{-9} = -6$
11. $(6.8) \div (-2.4) = -2.8\overline{3}$
12. $-72 \div (9) = -8$
13. $(-12) \div (9.9) = -1.\overline{21}$
14. $(-56) \div (8.0) = -7$
15. $(-\frac{2}{3}) \div (-18) = \frac{1}{27}$ or $0.\overline{037}$
16. $(-\frac{4}{5}) \div (-1.6) = \frac{1}{2}$ or 0.5
17. $(-\frac{3}{5}) \div (\frac{3}{5}) = -1$
18. $(-\frac{2}{3}) \div (36) = \frac{-1}{54}$
19. $(-3.4) \div (-9.99) = 0.\overline{340}$
20. $-21 \div (-9) = 2\frac{1}{3}$ or $2.\overline{3}$

Worksheet 2 (page 10)

Name_____
Operations with Real Numbers

Order of Operations

When solving an equation, be sure to follow the priority pyramid.

1. Parenthesis
2. Exponents
3. Multiplication & Division
4. Addition & Subtraction

Solve the following.

1. $3 + 2 \times 4 = 11$
2. $8 + 6 \times 2 = 20$
3. $7 + 5 - 8 = 4$
4. $4 + 10 \div 2 = 9$
5. $4^2 + 3^2 = 25$
6. $9 \div 3 \times 8 = 24$
7. $5(6 + 2) = 40$
8. $72 \div 8 \times 7 = 63$
9. $2 \times 15 \div 3 = 10$
10. $14 - 56 \div 7 = 6$
11. $9 - 3 + 6 = 12$
12. $6 + 3 - 2 = 7$
13. $32 \div 4 \times 3 = 24$
14. $2 \times 8 \div 4 = 4$
15. $12 - 30 \div 6 = 7$
16. $35 \div 5 - 6 = 1$
17. $5 \times 2 \times 8 = 80$
18. $15 - 60 \div 5 = 3$
19. $9 + 20 \div 5 = 13$
20. $6 - 40 \div 8 = 1$

Worksheet 3 (page 11)

Name_____
Operations with Real Numbers

Order of Operations

When solving an equation, be sure to follow the priority pyramid.

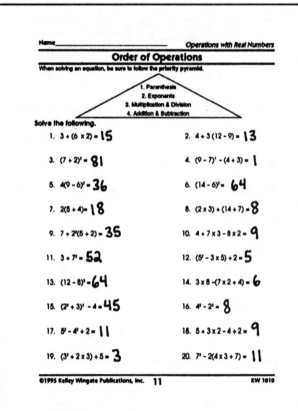

1. Parenthesis
2. Exponents
3. Multiplication & Division
4. Addition & Subtraction

Solve the following.

1. $3 + (6 \times 2) = 15$
2. $4 + 3(12 - 9) = 13$
3. $(7 + 2)^2 = 81$
4. $(9 - 7)^3 - (4 + 3) = 1$
5. $4(9 - 6)^2 = 36$
6. $(14 - 6)^2 = 64$
7. $2(5 + 4) = 18$
8. $(2 \times 3) + (14 + 7) = 8$
9. $7 + 2^2(5 + 2) = 35$
10. $4 + 7 \times 3 - 8 \times 2 = 9$
11. $3 + 7^2 = 52$
12. $(5^2 - 3 \times 5) + 2 = 5$
13. $(12 - 8)^3 = 64$
14. $3 \times 8 - (7 \times 2 + 4) = 6$
15. $(2^2 + 3)^2 - 4 = 45$
16. $4^2 - 2^2 = 8$
17. $5^2 - 4^2 + 2 = 11$
18. $5 + 3 \times 2 - 4 + 2 = 9$
19. $(3^2 + 2 \times 3) + 5 = 3$
20. $7^2 - 2(4 \times 3 + 7) = 11$

Worksheet 4 (page 12)

Name_____
Operations with Real Numbers

Order of Operations

When solving an equation, be sure to follow the priority pyramid.

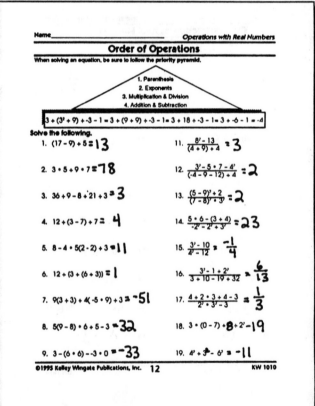

1. Parenthesis
2. Exponents
3. Multiplication & Division
4. Addition & Subtraction

$$3 + (3^2 \div 9) + -3 - 1 = 3 + (9 \div 9) + -3 - 1 = 3 + 18 \div -3 - 1 = 3 + -6 - 1 = -4$$

Solve the following.

1. $(17 - 9) + 5 = 13$
2. $3 \cdot 5 + 9 \cdot 7 = 78$
3. $36 \div 9 - 8 + 21 + 3 = 3$
4. $12 \div (3 - 7) + 7 = 4$
5. $8 - 4 \cdot 5(2 - 2) + 3 = 11$
6. $12 \div (3 + (6 + 3)) = 1$
7. $9(3 + 3) + 4(-5 + 9) + 3 = -51$
8. $5(9 - 8) + 6 + 5 - 3 = 32$
9. $3 - (6 \cdot 6) - 3 \cdot 0 = -33$
11. $\frac{8^2 - 13}{(4 + 9) \div 4} = 3$
12. $\frac{3^3 - 5 + 7 - 4^2}{(-4 - 9 - 12) \div 4} = 2$
13. $\frac{(5 - 9)^2 + 2}{(7 - 8)^2 + 3^3} = 2$
14. $\frac{5 + 6 - (3 + 4)}{-2^2 - 2^3 + 3^3} = 23$
15. $\frac{3^3 - 10}{4^3 - 12} = \frac{-1}{4}$
16. $\frac{3^3 - 1 + 2^3}{3 + 10 - 19 + 32} = \frac{6}{13}$
17. $\frac{4 + 2 + 3 + 4 - 3}{2^3 + 3^3 - 3} = \frac{1}{3}$
18. $3 \cdot (0 - 7) + 8 + 2^3 = -19$
19. $4^3 + 3^2 - 6^3 = -11$

Worksheet 13

Name_____ *Operations with Real Numbers*

Real Number Operations with absolute value

| -19 - 121 = -131 = -3 | 1-51 + 1-61 = 5 + 6 = 11 |

The absolute value of a number is its distance from zero.
For example: 151 = 5   1-61 = 6   101 = 0

Simplify the following.

1. 1-131 = **13**

2. -1 -81 = **-8**

3. 1-61 + 181 = **14**

4. 6 + 1-41 = **10**

5. 191 + 1-91 = **18**

6. -1-4 + 71 = **-3**

7. -1-5 + 91 = **-4**

8. 13 - 101 = **7**

9. -4 141 + 151 = **-11**

10. 141 - 161 = **-2**

11. 1231 - 1-121 = **11**

12. 1-91 + 1131 = **22**

13. 1131 - 1-151 = **-2**

14. 23 + 181 = **31**

15. 1231 + 9 = **32**

16. 1-651 - 1-171 = **48**

17. 141 - 1-121 - 4 = **-12**

18. 7 - 1-231 + 1-71 = **-9**

19. 111 - 101 + 6 = **7**

20. 1-171 - 1-171 = **0**

©1995 Kelley Wingate Publications, Inc.   13   KW 1010

Worksheet 14

Name_____ *Variables and Equations*

Substitution

Substitute and simplify.

a = 3, b = -9, c = 5

1. $a^2 + b^2 =$ **-720**

2. $(a + b)^2 =$ **36**

3. $a + b - c =$ **-11**

4. $(c - a)^2 =$ **4**

5. $2a - b - 3c =$ **0**

6. $(b + c)^2 =$ **16**

7. $b^2 + c^2 =$ **106**

8. $a^3 - (b + c)^2 =$ **11**

9. $-4b + (a + c)^2 =$ **100**

10. $abc =$ **-135**

Substitute and simplify.

a = -6, b = -3, c = 4

1. $3a - 4b =$ **-6**

2. $7c + b^2 =$ **1**

3. $a^2 - b^2 =$ **27**

4. $(a - b)^2 =$ **9**

5. $a^2 + b^2 =$ **45**

6. $(a + b)^2 =$ **81**

7. $c^2 - ab =$ **-2**

8. $2c + 3a - 4b =$ **2**

9. $a^2 - (b + c)^2 =$ **35**

10. $(a + b + c)^2 =$ **25**

©1995 Kelley Wingate Publications, Inc.   14   KW 1010

Worksheet 15

Name_____ *Variables and Equations*

Substitution

Substitute and simplify.

x = 2, y = 9, z = -5

1. $x + y + z =$ **6**

2. $8x + 3z =$ **1**

3. $4y + 3xz =$ **6**

4. $xyz + 10 =$ **-9**

5. $2(y + z) =$ **8**

6. $(y + z)^2 =$ **64**

7. $3z + xy =$ **3**

8. $(x + y + z)^2 =$ **36**

9. $(x + y)^2 =$ **121**

10. $(x - z) + y =$ **16**

Substitute and simplify.

w = -6, x = 4, y = 3, z = -8

1. $wx + yz =$ **-48**

2. $2w + 3z - xy + z^2 =$ **-560**

3. $y(z + x) =$ **-12**

4. $(w + x + y)^2 =$ **1**

5. $(z - w)^2 =$ **-8**

6. $5(w + x) + 4(y + z) =$ **-30**

7. $w^2 - x^2 =$ **20**

8. $(xy)^2 - 2wz =$ **48**

9. $wz - 4xy =$ **0**

10. $w + (x + y + z)^2 =$ **-5**

©1995 Kelley Wingate Publications, Inc.   15   KW 1010

Worksheet 16

Name_____ *Variables and Equations*

Combine Like Terms

| $9x + 7y + -21x = -12x + 7y$ |

Combine like terms.

1. $5x + 7x =$ **12x**

2. $19x + x =$ **20x**

3. $k - (-8k) =$ **9k**

4. $-12x + -4x =$ **-16x**

5. $13c - 12c =$ **1c**

6. $-e + 8e =$ **7e**

7. $3yz + 5yz =$ **8yz**

8. $-12n - -13n =$ **1n**

9. $12b + -34b =$ **-22b**

10. $13ab + (-12ab) =$ **1ab**

11. $4.7x - 5.9x =$ **-1.2x**

12. $7s + 5x - 8s =$ **-1s + 5x**

13. $4a + 9 + a =$ **5a + 9**

14. $5x - 6y - 8y + 7x =$ **12x - 14y**

15. $23x + 8 + 6x + 3y =$ **29x + 3y + 8**

16. $4xy + 7xy + 6x^2y + 7xy^2 =$
11xy + 6x²y + 7xy²

17. $2x - y + 2x + 3xy =$
4x - y + 3xy

18. $4x + 3y + -5y + 3xy + y =$
4x - y + 3xy

19. $2xy + 7x + 6xy + 3xy + -3x =$
11xy + 4x

20. $4x^2 + -7y + -4xy + 9x^2 + 2xy =$
13x² - 7y - 2xy

©1995 Kelley Wingate Publications, Inc.   16   KW 1010

Answer Key

Combine Like Terms

Name_____   *Variables and Equations*

$5(x + 3) + (4x - 7y) + (3x + 2y) = 5x + 15 + 4x - 7y + 3x + 2y = 12x + 15 - 5y$

Combine like terms.

1. $-2x + 3y - 5x - -8y + 9y$
$$-7x + 20y$$

2. $3x + (-3y) - (5x) + y$
$$-2x - 2y$$

3. $7 - 4y + x + 9y$
$$7 + x + 5y$$

4. $-21x + (-2x)$
$$-23x$$

5. $7(x - y) - 5(2x + 4y)$
$$-3x - 27y$$

6. $-n + 9n + 3 - 8 - 8n$
$$-5$$

7. $4(x + 5y) + 3(x + 6y) + 6(3x + 8y)$
$$25x + 86y$$

8. $12x + 6x + 9x - 3y - 7y + y$
$$27x - 9y$$

9. $-2(c - d) + (c - d) - 6(c - d)$
$$-7c + 7d$$

10. $-3(4x + -2y) - 2x(x + 3y) - 2(3x + 6y)$
$$-18x - 12y$$

11. $3(-4x + 7y) - 3x(2 + 3y)$
$$-18x - 9xy + 21y$$

12. $2y + 3(2y + 8x) - 3(8y + 2x)$
$$-16y + 18x$$

13. $5(3x^2 - 2y^2) + 3x(x + 3y^2)$
$$18x^2 + 9xy^2 - 10y^2$$

14. $2 + 4x + 3y - 4x + 7y$
$$-4xy$$

15. $3x + 4y + 2x + 5y - 4x$
$$x + 9y$$

16. $4(x + 5y) + (5x + y)$
$$9x + 21y$$

17. $5(x^2 + 3y^2) - y(x^2 + 5y)$
$$5x^2 - x^2y + 10y^2$$

18. $3(2(-y^2 + y) - 3) - 3(2x + y)$
$$-6y^2 + 3y - 9 - 6x$$

19. $4(x + 7y) - 2(2x + y)$
$$8x + 38y$$

20. $7x - 2y^2 + 3xy^2 + 2x^2 + 5xy^2$
$$2x^2 + 7x + 8xy^2 - 2y^2$$

Solving One-Step Equations (Addition and Subtraction)

Name_____   *Variables and Equations*

$$12 + x = -13$$
$$12 + -12 + x = -13 + -12$$
$$x = -25$$

Solve each equation for the given variable.

1. $y - 12 = 15$
$$y = 27$$

2. $x - 13 = -23$
$$x = -10$$

3. $12 + g = 14$
$$g = -2$$

4. $3 + x = 9$
$$x = 6$$

5. $-13 + x = 18$
$$x = 31$$

6. $-t + -7 = -56$
$$t = 49$$

7. $27 = v + -5$
$$v = 32$$

8. $-19 + b = 31$
$$b = 50$$

9. $a + 5.7 = 18.9$
$$a = 13.2$$

10. $-100 = b + -73$
$$b = -27$$

11. $-4 = x - 3$
$$x = -1$$

12. $2\frac{1}{3} + r = 4\frac{2}{6}$
$$r = 1\frac{8}{9}$$

13. $x + 2 = 2(3 - 4)$
$$x = -4$$

14. $-13 = n + (-36)$
$$n = 23$$

15. $c - 3 = 4.7$
$$c = 7.7$$

16. $r = 4.4 + 3.9$
$$r = 8.3$$

17. $z + 3.5 = 3.7$
$$z = 0.2$$

18. $s - 9 = (6 + -8)$
$$s = 7$$

19. $n + \frac{1}{2} = \frac{3}{4}$
$$n = \frac{1}{4}$$

20. $12 - -u = 19$
$$u = 7$$

Solving One-Step Equations Multiplication and Division)

Name_____   *Variables and Equations*

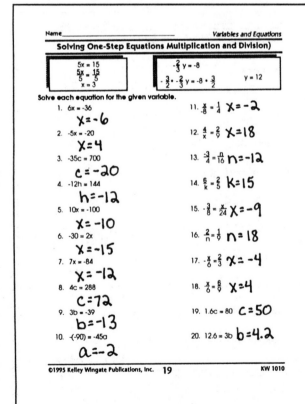

$$5x = 15$$
$$\frac{5x}{5} = \frac{15}{5}$$
$$x = 3$$

$$-\frac{2}{3}y = -8$$
$$-\frac{3}{2} \cdot -\frac{2}{3}y = -8 \cdot -\frac{3}{2}$$
$$y = 12$$

Solve each equation for the given variable.

1. $6x = -36$
$$x = -6$$

2. $-5x = -20$
$$x = 4$$

3. $-35c = 700$
$$c = -20$$

4. $-12h = 144$
$$h = -12$$

5. $10x = -100$
$$x = -10$$

6. $-30 = 2x$
$$x = -15$$

7. $7x = -84$
$$x = -12$$

8. $4c = 288$
$$c = 72$$

9. $3b = -39$
$$b = -13$$

10. $-(-90) = -45a$
$$a = -2$$

11. $\frac{x}{-8} = \frac{1}{4}$ $x = -2$

12. $\frac{4}{x} = \frac{2}{9}$ $x = 18$

13. $\frac{-3}{4} = \frac{n}{16}$ $n = -12$

14. $\frac{6}{k} = \frac{2}{5}$ $k = 15$

15. $-\frac{3}{8} = \frac{x}{24}$ $x = -9$

16. $\frac{2}{n} = \frac{1}{9}$ $n = 18$

17. $-\frac{x}{6} = \frac{2}{3}$ $x = -4$

18. $\frac{x}{6} = \frac{6}{9}$ $x = 4$

19. $1.6c = 80$ $c = 50$

20. $12.6 = 3b$ $b = 4.2$

Solving Basic Equations

Name_____   *Variables and Equations*

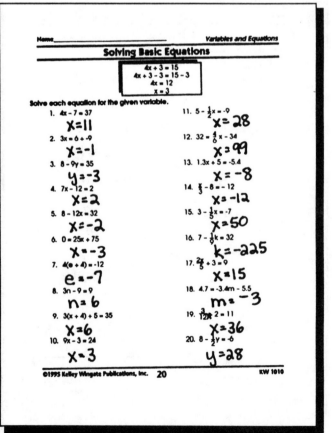

$$4x + 3 = 15$$
$$4x + 3 - 3 = 15 - 3$$
$$4x = 12$$
$$x = 3$$

Solve each equation for the given variable.

1. $4x - 7 = 37$
$$x = 11$$

2. $3x = 6 + -9$
$$x = -1$$

3. $8 - 9y = 35$
$$y = -3$$

4. $7x - 12 = 2$
$$x = 2$$

5. $8 - 12x = 32$
$$x = -2$$

6. $0 = 25x + 75$
$$x = -3$$

7. $4(e + 4) = -12$
$$e = -7$$

8. $3n - 9 = 9$
$$n = 6$$

9. $3(x + 4) + 5 = 35$
$$x = 6$$

10. $9x - 3 = 24$
$$x = 3$$

11. $5 - \frac{1}{2}x = -9$
$$x = 28$$

12. $32 = \frac{4}{6}x - 34$
$$x = 99$$

13. $1.3x + 5 = -5.4$
$$x = -8$$

14. $\frac{x}{3} - 8 = -12$
$$x = -12$$

15. $3 - \frac{1}{5}x = -7$
$$x = 50$$

16. $7 - \frac{1}{5}k = 32$
$$k = -225$$

17. $\frac{2x}{5} + 3 = 9$
$$x = 15$$

18. $4.7 = -3.4m - 5.5$
$$m = -3$$

19. $\frac{3}{12}x - 2 = 11$
$$x = 36$$

20. $8 - \frac{1}{2}y = -6$
$$y = 28$$

Answer Key

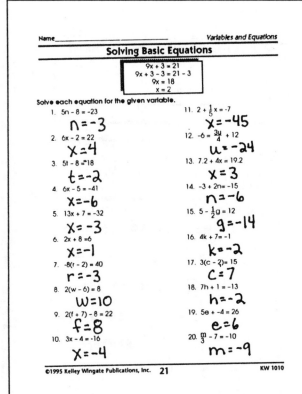

Name_____ Variables and Equations

Solving Basic Equations

$$9x + 3 = 21$$
$$9x + 3 - 3 = 21 - 3$$
$$9x = 18$$
$$x = 2$$

Solve each equation for the given variable.

1. $5n - 8 = -23$ → $n = -3$
2. $6x - 2 = 22$ → $x = 4$
3. $5t - 8 = -18$ → $t = -2$
4. $6x - 5 = -41$ → $x = -6$
5. $13x + 7 = -32$ → $x = -3$
6. $2x + 8 = 6$ → $x = -1$
7. $-8(r - 2) = 40$ → $r = -3$
8. $2(w - 6) = 8$ → $w = 10$
9. $2(f + 7) - 8 = 22$ → $f = 8$
10. $3x - 4 = -16$ → $x = -4$
11. $2 + \frac{1}{5}x = -7$ → $x = -45$
12. $-6 = \frac{3u}{4} + 12$ → $u = -24$
13. $7.2 + 4x = 19.2$ → $x = 3$
14. $-3 + 2n = -15$ → $n = -6$
15. $5 - \frac{1}{2}g = 12$ → $g = -14$
16. $4k + 7 = -1$ → $k = -2$
17. $3(c - 2) = 15$ → $c = 7$
18. $7h + 1 = -13$ → $h = -2$
19. $5e + -4 = 26$ → $e = 6$
20. $\frac{m}{3} - 7 = -10$ → $m = -9$

©1995 Kelley Wingate Publications, Inc.   21   KW 1010

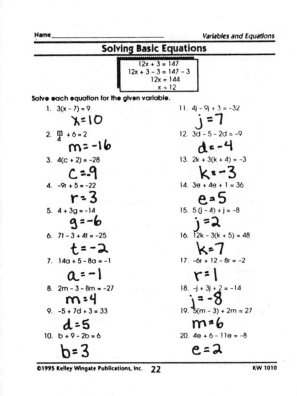

Name_____ Variables and Equations

Solving Basic Equations

$$12x + 3 = 147$$
$$12x + 3 - 3 = 147 - 3$$
$$12x = 144$$
$$x = 12$$

Solve each equation for the given variable.

1. $3(x - 7) = 9$ → $x = 10$
2. $\frac{m}{4} + 6 = 2$ → $m = -16$
3. $4(c + 2) = -28$ → $c = 9$
4. $-9r + 5 = -22$ → $r = 3$
5. $4 + 3g = -14$ → $g = -6$
6. $7t - 3 + 4t = -25$ → $t = -2$
7. $14a + 5 - 8a = -1$ → $a = -1$
8. $2m - 3 - 8m = -27$ → $m = 4$
9. $-5 + 7d + 3 = 33$ → $d = 5$
10. $b + 9 - 2b = 6$ → $b = 3$
11. $4j - 9j + 3 = -32$ → $j = 7$
12. $3d - 5 - 2d = -9$ → $d = -4$
13. $2k + 3(k + 4) = -3$ → $k = -3$
14. $3e + 4e + 1 = 36$ → $e = 5$
15. $5(j - 4) + j = -8$ → $j = 2$
16. $12k - 3(k + 5) = 48$ → $k = 7$
17. $-6r + 12 - 8r = -2$ → $r = 1$
18. $-j + 3j + 2 = -14$ → $j = -8$
19. $5(m - 3) + 2m = 27$ → $m = 6$
20. $4e + 6 - 11e = -8$ → $e = 2$

©1995 Kelley Wingate Publications, Inc.   22   KW 1010

Name_____ Variables and Equations

Solving Equations with Variables on Both Sides

$$6x - 7 = x + 23$$
$$6x - x - 7 = x - x + 23$$
$$5x - 7 = 23$$
$$5x = 30$$
$$x = 6$$

Solve each equation for the given variable.

1. $2x - 7 = 3x + 4$ → $x = -11$
2. $-7c + 9 = c + 1$ → $c = 1$
3. $4(2y - 4) = 5y + 2$ → $y = 6$
4. $-6 - 2n = 3n - (6 + 5)$ → $n = 5$
5. $4(t + 5) - 3 = 6t - 13$ → $t = 15$
6. $2(r - 4) = 5(r + -7)$ → $r = 9$
7. $7 - 6a = 6 - 7a$ → $a = -1$
8. $12m - 9 = 4m + 15$ → $m = 3$
9. $8(x - 3) + 8 = 5x - 22$ → $x = -2$
10. $3c - 12 = 14 + 5c$ → $c = -13$
11. $9a + 5 = 3a - 1$ → $a = -1$
12. $6(x - 9) = 4(x - 5)$ → $x = 17$
13. $2(x - 4) + 8 = 3x - 8$ → $x = 8$
14. $3x - 3 = -3x + -3$ → $x = 0$
15. $-10x + 6 = -7x + -9$ → $x = 5$
16. $5 + 3x = 7(x + 3)$ → $x = -4$
17. $\frac{5}{2}x + 3 = \frac{1}{2}x + 15$ → $x = 6$
18. $2x + 6 = 5x - 9$ → $x = 5$
19. $4e - 19 = -3(e + 4)$ → $e = 1$
20. $5t + 7 = 4t - 9$ → $t = -16$

©1995 Kelley Wingate Publications, Inc.   23   KW 1010

Name_____ Variables and Equations

Problem Solving

The sum of three times a number and 45 is 67. Find the number.

$$3x + 45 = 66$$
$$3x + 45 - 45 = 66 - 45$$
$$3x = 21$$
$$x = 7 \quad \text{The number is 7.}$$

Write an equation for each word problem and solve it.

1. The sum of 4 times a number and 5 is -7. Find the number.
   Equation: $4x + 5 = -7$
   Solution: $x = -3$
2. The difference of 5 times a number and 6 is 14. Find the number.
   Equation: $5x - 6 = 14$
   Solution: $x = 4$
3. The product of a number and 5 is 80. Find the number.
   Equation: $5x = 80$
   Solution: $x = 16$
4. Twice a number added to 7 is 13. Find the number.
   Equation: $2x + 7 = 13$
   Solution: $x = 3$
5. The sum of a number and -6 is 4. Find the number.
   Equation: $x + -6 = 4$
   Solution: $x = 10$
6. The difference of a number and -3 is 8. Find the number.
   Equation: $x - (-3) = 8$
   Solution: $x = 5$
7. 12 subtracted from 3 times a number is 15. Find the number.
   Equation: $3x - 12 = 15$
   Solution: $x = 9$
8. The quotient of a number and 4 is -8. Find the number.
   Equation: $\frac{x}{4} = -8 \;/\; x = -32$
   Solution:

©1995 Kelley Wingate Publications, Inc.   24   KW 1010

Answer Key

Variables and Equations

Problem Solving

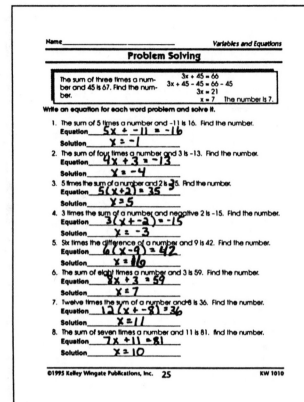

The sum of three times a number and 45 is 67. Find the number.

$3x + 45 = 66$
$3x + 45 - 45 = 66 - 45$
$3x = 21$
$x = 7$ The number is 7.

Write an equation for each word problem and solve it.

1. The sum of 5 times a number and -11 is 16. Find the number.
   Equation___$5x + -11 = -16$___
   Solution___$x = -1$___

2. The sum of four times a number and 3 is -13. Find the number.
   Equation___$4x + 3 = -13$___
   Solution___$x = -4$___

3. 5 times the sum of a number and 2 is 35. Find the number.
   Equation___$5(x+2) = 35$___
   Solution___$x = 5$___

4. 3 times the sum of a number and negative 2 is -15. Find the number.
   Equation___$3(x+-2) = -15$___
   Solution___$x = -3$___

5. Six times the difference of a number and 9 is 42. Find the number.
   Equation___$6(x-9) = 42$___
   Solution___$x = 16$___

6. The sum of eight times a number and 3 is 59. Find the number.
   Equation___$8x + 3 = 59$___
   Solution___$x = 7$___

7. Twelve times the sum of a number and 8 is 36. Find the number.
   Equation___$12(x + -8) = 36$___
   Solution___$x = 11$___

8. The sum of seven times a number and 11 is 81. Find the number.
   Equation___$7x + 11 = 81$___
   Solution___$x = 10$___

Variables and Equations

Solving Inequalities with Multiple Operations

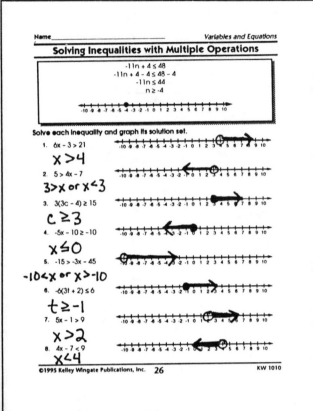

$-11n + 4 \leq 48$
$-11n + 4 - 4 \leq 48 - 4$
$-11n \leq 44$
$n \geq -4$

Solve each inequality and graph its solution set.

1. $6x - 3 > 21$
   $x > 4$

2. $5 > 4x - 7$
   $3 > x$ or $x < 3$

3. $3(3c - 4) \geq 15$
   $c \geq 3$

4. $-5x - 10 \geq -10$
   $x \leq 0$

5. $-15 > -3x - 45$
   $-10 < x$ or $x > -10$

6. $-6(3t + 2) \leq 6$
   $t \geq -1$

7. $5x - 1 > 9$
   $x > 2$

8. $4x - 7 < 9$
   $x < 4$

Variables and Equations

Solving Inequalities with Variables on Both Sides

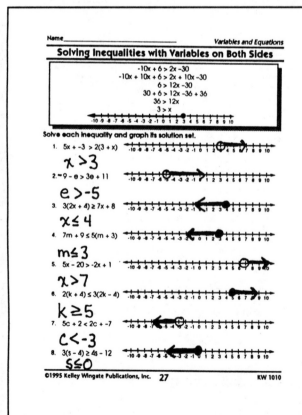

$-10x + 6 > 2x - 30$
$-10x + 10x + 6 > 2x + 10x - 30$
$6 > 12x - 30$
$30 + 6 > 12x - 36 + 36$
$36 > 12x$
$3 > x$

Solve each inequality and graph its solution set.

1. $5x + -3 > 2(3 + x)$
   $x > 3$

2. $-9 - e > 3e + 11$
   $e > -5$

3. $3(2x + 4) \geq 7x + 8$
   $x \leq 4$

4. $7m + 9 \leq 5(m + 3)$
   $m \leq 3$

5. $5x - 20 > -2x + 1$
   $x > 7$

6. $2(k + 4) \leq 3(2k - 4)$
   $k \geq 5$

7. $5c + 2 < 2c + -7$
   $c < -3$

8. $3(s - 4) \geq 4s - 12$
   $s \leq 0$

Variables and Equations

Practice Solving Inequalities

Solve each inequality and graph its solution set.

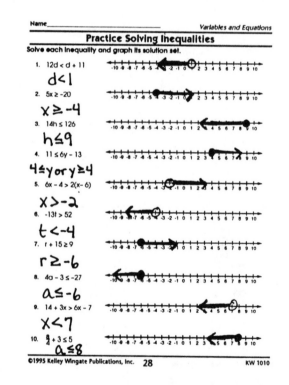

1. $12d < d + 11$
   $d < 1$

2. $5x \geq -20$
   $x \geq -4$

3. $14h \leq 126$
   $h \leq 9$

4. $11 \leq 6y - 13$
   $4 \leq y$ or $y \geq 4$

5. $6x - 4 > 2(x - 6)$
   $x > -2$

6. $-13t > 52$
   $t < -4$

7. $r + 15 \geq 9$
   $r \geq -6$

8. $4a - 3 \leq -27$
   $a \leq -6$

9. $14 + 3x > 6x - 7$
   $x < 7$

10. $\frac{a}{8} + 3 \leq 5$
    $a \leq 8$

Answer Key

Worksheet 1 (page 29)

Name_____   Variables and Equations

Practice Solving Inequalities

Solve each inequality and graph its solution set.

1. $4w > 2w + 6$

$w > 3$

2. $5n + 3 \geq -12$

$n > -3$

3. $-2a < 5 + 3a$

$a > -1$

4. $-3.6 > 0.6x$

$x < -6$

5. $13x \geq -39$

$x \geq -3$

6. $6d < 3d - 18$

$d < -6$

7. $7c - 8 \geq 6$

$c \geq 2$

8. $15e - 3 \leq 20e + 12$

$e \geq -3$

9. $7k < -28$

$k < -4$

10. $4 + 6r > -8$

$r > -2$

©1995 Kelley Wingate Publications, Inc.   29   KW 1010

Worksheet 2 (page 30)

Name_____   Polynomials

Adding and Subtracting Polynomials

$$(x^2 + 3x + 1) - (3x^2 + 4x - 7) = 4x^2 - x + 8$$

Add or subtract the following polynomials by combining like terms.

1. $(-2x^2 + 4x - 12) + (5x^2 - 5x) = 3x^2 - x - 12$

2. $(3y^2 - 9y) - (-5y^2 + 7y - 7) = 8y^2 - 16y + 7$

3. $(3x^4 - 2x + 1) - (4x^3 - 5x - 8) = 3x^4 - 4x^3 + 3x + 9$

4. $(6x^3 - 2x^2 - 12) + (6x^3 + 3x + 8) = 6x^3 + 4x^2 + 3x - 4$

5. $(x^2 - x - 4) - (3x^2 - 4x + 5) = 2x^2 + 3x - 9$

6. $(x^3 - x^2 + 3) - (4x^3 - x^2 + 7) = -3x^3 - 4$

7. $(4x^2 + 6x + 3) + (3x^2 - 3x - 2) + (-4x^2 + 3x - 9) = 3x^2 + 6x - 8$

8. $(7x^2 + 2x + 7) - (4x^2 - 2x + 3) + (-5x^2 + 6x + 7) = -2x^2 + 10x + 11$

9. $(3x^3 - 5x^2 - 9) - (5x^3 - 5x - 4) - (5x^3 - 4x^2 - 9) = -7x^3 - x^2 + 5x + 4$

10. $(2x^3 - 9x - 8) - (2x^3 - 4x^2 + -2) = -2x^3 + 6x^2 - 9x - 6$

11. $(9x^3 - 8x + -4) + (3x^3 - 7x + -5) + (-4x^2 - 2x + -6) = 3x^3 + 5x^2 - 17x - 15$

12. $(3x^3 + 3x + 2) - (5x^3 - 3x^2 + 8) - (-2x^3 + 9x^2 + 8) = -3x^3 - 3x^2 + 3x - 14$

13. $(-2x^3 + 3x^2 + 9) + (-8x^3 - 2x^2 - 4x) = -10x^3 + x^2 - 4x + 9$

14. $(-6x^3 - 3x^2 + 4) + (-7x^3 + 2x + 4) - (-3x^3 + 5x^2 + 2) = -7x^3 - 11x^2 + 2x + 6$

15. $(-3x^2 - 4x^2 - 1) - (2x^3 - 7x - 9) - (2x^3 - 2x^2 - 3) = -8x^2 - x^2 + 7x + 11$

©1995 Kelley Wingate Publications, Inc.   30   KW 1010

Worksheet 3 (page 31)

Name_____   Polynomials

Raising Exponents to a Power

RULE: $(x^a)^b = x^{ab}$ $(x^a y^b)^c = x^{ac} y^{bc}$

Multiply the following polynomials.

1. $(xy^2)(x^3y) = x^4 y^4$

2. $(7xy^2)(-5x^3y^3) = -35x^4 y^5$

3. $(x^3y^3)^3 = x^9 y^9$

4. $(-4x^3y^3)^3 = 256 x^{12} y^{12}$

5. $(6x^5y^4)^3 = 216 x^{15} y^{12}$

6. $(x^3y^3)(x^2y^2) = x^5 y^5$

7. $(-9xy^3)^3 = -729 x^3 y^9$

8. $(-4x^4y^5)^3 = -64 x^{12} y^{15}$

9. $(x^3y) = x^6 y^2$

10. $(3xy^3)^2(-4x^2y^2)^2(2xy^3) =$

$288 x^7 y^{17}$

11. $(-2x^2y^3)^2 = 4x^4 y^6$

12. $(5x^2y^4)^3 = 125 x^6 y^{12}$

13. $(-6xy^3)^3 = -216 x^{12} y^{18}$

14. $(7xy)^2 = 49 x^2 y^2$

15. $(-3x^3y)^3 = -27 x^9 y^3$

16. $(-2x^2y)^3 = -8x^6 y^3$

17. $(4x^2y^3)^2 = 256 x^8 y^{12}$

18. $(2x)^5 = 32 x^5$

19. $(6x^2y^3)^0 = 1$

20. $(-3x^2y)^4 = 81 x^8 y^4$

©1995 Kelley Wingate Publications, Inc.   31   KW 1010

Worksheet 4 (page 32)

Name_____   Polynomials

Multiplying Exponents

Rule: $x^a \cdot x^b = x^{a+b}$ Example: $a^4 \cdot a^3 = a^7$

Multiply the following polynomials.

1. $a \cdot a^2 \cdot a^3 = a^6$

2. $(2a^2b)(4ab^2) = 8a^3 b^3$

3. $(6x^2)(-3x^5) = -18 x^7$

4. $b^3 \cdot b^4 \cdot b^2 \cdot b = b^{15}$

5. $(3x^3)(3x^3)(-3x^3) = -27 x^9$

6. $(4c^2)(-8c^7) = -32 c^9$

7. $(5xy)(2x^2y^3) = 10 x^3 y^4$

8. $(3x)(-4y^3)(6x^3y) = -72 x^4 y^3$

9. $(-2c^2)(6cd)(-cd^2) = 12 c^6 d^3$

10. $(6k^2)(-3k)(2k^5) = -36 k^8$

11. $(m^2n)(mn^2)(mn) = m^4 n^5$

12. $(-4p^5)(-3p^6)(-2p^7) = -24 p^{18}$

13. $(12e^3)(2g)(4eh) = 96 e^4 g^3 h$

14. $(5f)(-3f^2)(2f) = -30 f^5$

15. $(c^2h)(ch)(c^3h^6) = c^6 h^8$

16. $(3c^2d^3)(-5cd^3) = -15 c^3 d^6$

17. $(5x^2y^3)(x^4y)(-x^2y^2) = -5x^7 y^6$

18. $(-4m^3)(-4m^3) = 16 m^6$

19. $d \cdot d^2 \cdot d^3 \cdot d^4 \cdot d^5 = d^{15}$

20. $(-1)(x)(-x^2)(x)(-x^2) = -x^6$

©1995 Kelley Wingate Publications, Inc.   32   KW 1010

Dividing Exponents

Name_____   Polynomials

Rule: $\frac{x^a}{x^b} = x^{a-b}$ Example: $\frac{x^5}{x^4} = x^1$ $\frac{x^7}{x^3} = x^{7-3} = x^4$

Divide the following polynomials.

1. $\frac{x^4}{x^2} = x^2$
2. $\frac{-9a^3b^4}{-3ab} = -3a^2b^3$
3. $\frac{d^4}{d^2} = d^2$
4. $\frac{b^{11}c^7}{b^2c^2} = b^9c^5$
5. $\frac{-12m^5}{6m} = -2m^4$
6. $\frac{15k^5r^4}{-3k^3r} = -5k^2r^3$
7. $\frac{9a^{11}}{a^1} = 9a^{10}$
8. $\frac{(3xy)(4x^2y)}{-6xy^2} = -2x^2$
9. $\frac{-14c^7d^4}{-2c^1d^2} = 7c^6d^2$
10. $\frac{(5k)(-8k^3)}{10k^3} = -4k^3$
11. $\frac{18c^3}{-3c^2} = -6c$
12. $\frac{-48c^5d^4}{-8cd} = 6cd^3$
13. $\frac{22y^5z^3}{2yz^2} = 11y^4z$
14. $\frac{28x^3y}{-4x^3} = -7y$
15. $\frac{-3p^8}{6p^2} = -\frac{p^6}{2}$
16. $\frac{42k^{11}}{-7k^6} = -6r^5$
17. $\frac{(6x^3)(4x^3)}{-12x^4} = -2x^2$
18. $\frac{21k^6}{(3k)(7k^1)} = k^4$
19. $\frac{4x^3y^3z^2}{2xy^2z} = 2xyz$
20. $\frac{(121c^7)(-c^2)}{11c^3} = -11c^6$

KW 1010

Negative Exponents

Name_____   Polynomials

Rule: $x^{-a} = \frac{1}{x^a}$ Example: $3^{-2} = \frac{1}{9}$ $8x^{-2} = \frac{8}{x^2}$ $(4x)^{-3} = \frac{1}{64x^3}$

Simplify the following.

1. $a^{-6} = \frac{1}{a^6}$
2. $2^{-4} = \frac{1}{16}$
3. $b^{-5} = \frac{1}{b^5}$
4. $\left(\frac{2}{3}\right)^{-1} = \frac{3}{2}$
5. $c^{-9} = \frac{1}{c^9}$
6. $(xy)^{-1} = \frac{1}{xy}$
7. $\left(\frac{3}{4}\right)^{-2} = \frac{16}{9}$
8. $(2x)^{-3} = \frac{1}{8x^3}$
9. $(c^2d)^{-1} = \frac{1}{c^2d}$
10. $(6y^2)^{-2} = \frac{1}{36y^4}$
11. $7x^{-3} = \frac{7}{x^3}$
12. $m^2n^{-2} = \frac{m^2}{n^2}$
13. $3a^2b^{-3} = \frac{3a^2}{b^3}$
14. $-2x^{-3} = \frac{-2}{x^3}$
15. $(-11xy)^{-2} = \frac{1}{121x^2y^2}$
16. $(-3)^{-3} = \frac{1}{-27}$
17. $5cd^{-9} = \frac{5c}{d^9}$
18. $(-3x^2)^{-3} = \frac{1}{9x^6}$
19. $12x^{-8}y = \frac{12y}{x^8}$
20. $\left(\frac{x^2}{y^3}\right)^{-2} = \frac{y^6}{x^4}$

KW 1010

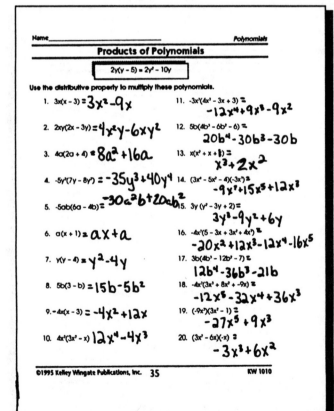

Products of Polynomials

Name_____   Polynomials

$2y(y - 5) = 2y^2 - 10y$

Use the distributive property to multiply these polynomials.

1. $3x(x - 3) = 3x^2 - 9x$
2. $2xy(2x - 3y) = 4x^2y - 6xy^2$
3. $4a(2a + 4) = 8a^2 + 16a$
4. $-5y^2(7y - 8y) = -35y^3 + 40y^4$
5. $-5ab(6a - 4b) = -30a^2b + 20ab^2$
6. $a(x + 1) = ax + a$
7. $y(y - 4) = y^2 - 4y$
8. $5b(3 - b) = 15b - 5b^2$
9. $-4x(x - 3) = -4x^2 + 12x$
10. $4x^2(3x^2 - x) = 12x^4 - 4x^3$
11. $-3x^2(4x^2 - 3x + 3) = -12x^4 + 9x^3 - 9x^2$
12. $5b(4b^3 - 6b^2 - 6) = 20b^4 - 30b^3 - 30b$
13. $x(x^2 + x + 1) = x^3 + 2x^2$
14. $(3x^2 - 5x^2 - 4)(-3x^2) = -9x^7 + 15x^5 + 12x^3$
15. $3y(y^2 - 3y + 2) = 3y^3 - 9y^2 + 6y$
16. $-4x^2(5 - 3x + 3x^2 + 4x^3) = -20x^2 + 12x^3 - 12x^4 - 16x^5$
17. $3b(4b^3 - 12b^2 + 7) = 12b^4 - 36b^3 - 21b$
18. $-4x^2(3x^3 + 8x^2 + -9x) = -12x^5 - 32x^4 + 36x^3$
19. $(-9x^2)(3x^3 - 1) = -27x^5 + 9x^3$
20. $(3x^2 - 6x)(-x) = -3x^3 + 6x^2$

KW 1010

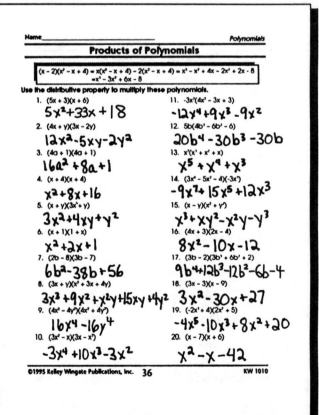

Products of Polynomials

Name_____   Polynomials

$(x - 2)(x^2 - x + 4) = x(x^2 - x + 4) - 2(x^2 - x + 4) = x^3 - x^2 + 4x - 2x^2 + 2x - 8$
$= x^3 - 3x^2 + 6x - 8$

Use the distributive property to multiply these polynomials.

1. $(5x + 3)(x + 6) = 5x^2 + 33x + 18$
2. $(4x + y)(3x - 2y) = 12x^2 - 5xy - 2y^2$
3. $(4a + 1)(4a + 1) = 16a^2 + 8a + 1$
4. $(x + 4)(x + 4) = x^2 + 8x + 16$
5. $(x + y)(3x + y) = 3x^2 + 4xy + y^2$
6. $(x + 1)(1 + x) = x^2 + 2x + 1$
7. $(2b - 8)(3b - 7) = 6b^2 - 38b + 56$
8. $(3x + y)(x^2 + 3x + 4y) = 3x^3 + 9x^2 + x^2y + 15xy + 4y^2$
9. $(4x^2 - 4y^2)(4x^2 + 4y^2) = 16x^4 - 16y^4$
10. $(3x^2 - x)(3x - x^2) = -3x^4 + 10x^3 - 3x^2$
11. $-3x^2(4x^2 - 3x + 3) = -12x^4 + 9x^3 - 9x^2$
12. $5b(4b^3 - 6b^2 - 6) = 20b^4 - 30b^3 - 30b$
13. $x^2(x^3 + x^2 + x) = x^5 + x^4 + x^3$
14. $(3x^2 - 5x^2 - 4)(-3x^2) = -9x^7 + 15x^5 + 12x^3$
15. $(x - y)(x^2 + y) = x^3 + xy^2 - x^2y - y^3$
16. $(4x + 3)(2x - 4) = 8x^2 - 10x - 12$
17. $(3b - 2)(3b^2 + 6b^2 + 2) = 9b^4 + 12b^3 - 12b^2 - 6b - 4$
18. $(3x - 3)(x - 9) = 3x^2 - 30x + 27$
19. $(-2x^2 + 4)(2x^3 + 5) = -4x^5 - 10x^3 + 8x^2 + 20$
20. $(x - 7)(x + 6) = x^2 - x - 42$

KW 1010

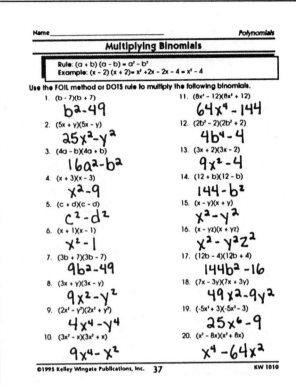

Name_____ *Polynomials*

Multiplying Binomials

Rule: $(a + b)(a - b) = a^2 - b^2$
Example: $(x - 2)(x + 2) = x^2 + 2x - 2x - 4 = x^2 - 4$

Use the FOIL method or DOTS rule to multiply the following binomials.

1. $(b - 7)(b + 7)$
$b^2 - 49$

2. $(5x + y)(5x - y)$
$25x^2 - y^2$

3. $(4a - b)(4a + b)$
$16a^2 - b^2$

4. $(x + 3)(x - 3)$
$x^2 - 9$

5. $(c + d)(c - d)$
$c^2 - d^2$

6. $(x + 1)(x - 1)$
$x^2 - 1$

7. $(3b + 7)(3b - 7)$
$9b^2 - 49$

8. $(3x + y)(3x - y)$
$9x^2 - y^2$

9. $(2x^2 - y^2)(2x^2 + y^2)$
$4x^4 - y^4$

10. $(3x^2 - x)(3x^2 + x)$
$9x^4 - x^2$

11. $(8x^2 - 12)(8x^2 + 12)$
$64x^4 - 144$

12. $(2b^2 - 2)(2b^2 + 2)$
$4b^4 - 4$

13. $(3x + 2)(3x - 2)$
$9x^2 - 4$

14. $(12 + b)(12 - b)$
$144 - b^2$

15. $(x - y)(x + y)$
$x^2 - y^2$

16. $(x - yz)(x + yz)$
$x^2 - y^2z^2$

17. $(12b - 4)(12b + 4)$
$144b^2 - 16$

18. $(7x - 3y)(7x + 3y)$
$49x^2 - 9y^2$

19. $(-5x^3 + 3)(-5x^3 - 3)$
$25x^6 - 9$

20. $(x^2 - 8x)(x^2 + 8x)$
$x^4 - 64x^2$

©1995 Kelley Wingate Publications, Inc. 37 KW 1010

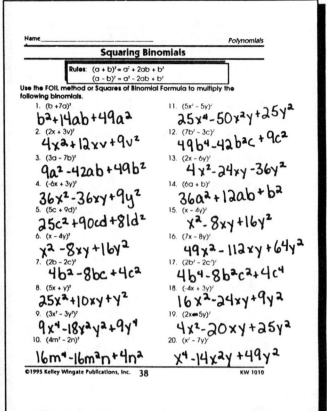

Name_____ *Polynomials*

Squaring Binomials

Rules: $(a + b)^2 = a^2 + 2ab + b^2$
$(a - b)^2 = a^2 - 2ab + b^2$

Use the FOIL method or Squares of Binomial Formula to multiply the following binomials.

1. $(b + 7a)^2$
$b^2 + 14ab + 49a^2$

2. $(2x + 3y)^2$
$4x^2 + 12xy + 9y^2$

3. $(3a - 7b)^2$
$9a^2 - 42ab + 49b^2$

4. $(-6x + 3y)^2$
$36x^2 - 36xy + 9y^2$

5. $(5c + 9d)^2$
$25c^2 + 90cd + 81d^2$

6. $(x - 4y)^2$
$x^2 - 8xy + 16y^2$

7. $(2b - 2c)^2$
$4b^2 - 8bc + 4c^2$

8. $(5x + y)^2$
$25x^2 + 10xy + y^2$

9. $(3x^2 - 3y^2)^2$
$9x^4 - 18x^2y^2 + 9y^4$

10. $(4m^2 - 2n)^2$
$16m^4 - 16m^2n + 4n^2$

11. $(5x^2 - 5y)^2$
$25x^4 - 50x^2y + 25y^2$

12. $(7b^2 - 3c)^2$
$49b^4 - 42b^2c + 9c^2$

13. $(2x - 6y)^2$
$4x^2 - 24xy - 36y^2$

14. $(6a + b)^2$
$36a^2 + 12ab + b^2$

15. $(x - 4y)^2$
$x^2 - 8xy + 16y^2$

16. $(7x - 8y)^2$
$49x^2 - 112xy + 64y^2$

17. $(2b^2 - 2c^2)^2$
$4b^4 - 8b^2c^2 + 4c^4$

18. $(-4x + 3y)^2$
$16x^2 - 24xy + 9y^2$

19. $(2x - 5y)^2$
$4x^2 - 20xy + 25y^2$

20. $(x^2 - 7y)^2$
$x^4 - 14x^2y + 49y^2$

©1995 Kelley Wingate Publications, Inc. 38 KW 1010

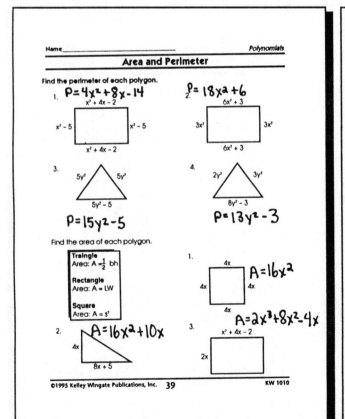

Name_____ *Polynomials*

Area and Perimeter

Find the perimeter of each polygon.

1. $P = 4x^2 + 8x - 14$
rectangle: top $x^2 + 4x - 2$, sides $x^2 - 5$, $x^2 - 5$, bottom $x^2 + 4x - 2$

2. $P = 18x^2 + 6$
rectangle: top $6x^2 + 3$, sides $3x^2$, $3x^2$, bottom $6x^2 + 3$

3. triangle: $5y^2$, $5y^2$, $5y^2 - 5$
$P = 15y^2 - 5$

4. triangle: $2y^2$, $3y^2$, $8y^2 - 3$
$P = 13y^2 - 3$

Find the area of each polygon.

Traingle Area: $A = \frac{1}{2}bh$
Rectangle Area: $A = LW$
Square Area: $A = s^2$

1. square $4x$: $A = 16x^2$

2. triangle $4x$ by $8x + 5$: $A = 16x^2 + 10x$

3. rectangle $x^2 + 4x - 2$ by $2x$: $A = 2x^3 + 8x^2 - 4x$

©1995 Kelley Wingate Publications, Inc. 39 KW 1010

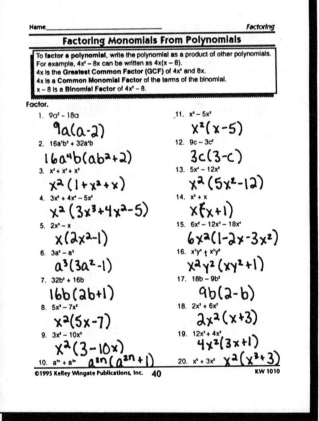

Name_____ *Factoring*

Factoring Monomials From Polynomials

To factor a polynomial, write the polynomial as a product of other polynomials.
For example, $4x^2 - 8x$ can be written as $4x(x - 8)$.
$4x$ is the **Greatest Common Factor (GCF)** of $4x^2$ and $8x$.
$4x$ is a **Common Monomial Factor** of the terms of the binomial.
$x - 8$ is a **Binomial Factor** of $4x^2 - 8$.

Factor.

1. $9a^2 - 18a$
$9a(a - 2)$

2. $16a^3b^3 + 32a^2b$
$16a^2b(ab^2 + 2)$

3. $x^2 + x^3 + x^4$
$x^2(1 + x^2 + x)$

4. $3x^4 + 4x^4 - 5x^2$
$x^2(3x^3 + 4x^2 - 5)$

5. $2x^3 - x$
$x(2x^2 - 1)$

6. $3a^5 - a^3$
$a^3(3a^2 - 1)$

7. $32b^2 + 16b$
$16b(2b + 1)$

8. $5x^3 - 7x^2$
$x^2(5x - 7)$

9. $3x^2 - 10x^3$
$x^2(3 - 10x)$

10. $a^{4n} + a^{2n}$
$a^{2n}(a^{2n} + 1)$

11. $x^3 - 5x^2$
$x^2(x - 5)$

12. $9c - 3c^2$
$3c(3 - c)$

13. $5x^4 - 12x^2$
$x^2(5x^2 - 12)$

14. $x^2 + x$
$x(x + 1)$

15. $6x^2 - 12x^3 - 18x^4$
$6x^2(1 - 2x - 3x^2)$

16. $x^3y^4 + x^2y^2$
$x^2y^2(xy^2 + 1)$

17. $18b - 9b^3$
$9b(2 - b)$

18. $2x^3 + 6x^2$
$2x^2(x + 3)$

19. $12x^3 + 4x^2$
$4x^2(3x + 1)$

20. $x^5 + 3x^2$
$x^2(x^3 + 3)$

©1995 Kelley Wingate Publications, Inc. 40 KW 1010

Worksheet 41

Name_____ *Factoring*

Factoring Trinomials of the form x² + bx + c

$$a^2 - 8a + 15 = (a - 5)(a - 3)$$

Factor.

1. $x^2 - 8x + 16$
$(x-4)(x-4)$

2. $x^2 - 12x + 20$
$(x-10)(x-2)$

3. $x^2 - 12x + 11$
$(x-11)(x-1)$

4. $c^2 + c - 20$
$(c+5)(c-4)$

5. $x^2 + 12x + 36$
$(x+6)(x+6)$

6. $x^2 - x - 6$
$(x-3)(x+2)$

7. $x^2 + 12x + 35$
$(x+7)(x+5)$

8. $x^2 - 9x + 18$
$(x-6)(x-3)$

9. $y^2 - 13y + 42$
$(y-6)(y-7)$

10. $x^2 + 6x - 40$
$(x+10)(x-4)$

11. $x^2 + x - 132$
$(x+12)(x-11)$

12. $x^2 - 8xy + 33y^2$
$(x-11y)(x+3y)$

13. $a^2 - 10ab - 24b^2$
$(a-12b)(a+2b)$

14. $m^2 - 3mn + 2n^2$
$(m-n)(m-2n)$

15. $x^2 + 15xy + 44y^2$
$(x+11y)(x+4y)$

16. $t^2 + 23t + 42$
$(t+21)(t+2)$

17. $y^2 - 12y + 36$
$(y-6)(y-6)$

18. $b^2 - 4b - 45$
$(b-9)(b+5)$

19. $n^2 + 3n - 18$
$(n+6)(n-3)$

20. $c^2 - 10c + 21$
$(c-7)(c-3)$

©1995 Kelley Wingate Publications, Inc.   41   KW 1010

Worksheet 42

Name_____ *Factoring*

Factoring Trinomials of the form x² + bx + c

$$x^2 + 3x - 28 = (x + 7)(x - 4)$$

Factor.

1. $x^2 + 4x - 5$
$(x+5)(x-1)$

2. $x^2 + 15x + 50$
$(x+10)(x+5)$

3. $x^2 + 4x - 32$
$(x+8)(x-4)$

4. $x^2 + 7x + 6$
$(x+6)(x+1)$

5. $x^2 + 12x + 11$
$(x+11)(x+1)$

6. $x^2 + 12x + 20$
$(x+10)(x+2)$

7. $x^2 + 2x - 35$
$(x+7)(x-5)$

8. $x^2 - 18x + 72$
$(x-6)(x-12)$

9. $x^2 - 15x + 56$
$(x-8)(x-7)$

10. $x^2 - 6x - 16$
$(x-8)(x+2)$

11. $x^2 - 8x + 15$
$(x-5)(x-3)$

12. $x^2 + x - 72$
$(x+9)(x-8)$

13. $x^2 - 16x + 39$
$(x-13)(x-3)$

14. $x^2 + 22x + 121$
$(x+11)(x+11)$

15. $x^2 + 13x + 12$
$(x+12)(x+1)$

16. $x^2 - 3xy + 2y^2$
$(x-y)(x-2y)$

17. $x^2 - 14xy + 24y^2$
$(x-12y)(x-2y)$

18. $x^2 + 5xy + 6y^2$
$(x+2y)(x+3y)$

19. $x^2 + 2xy - 63y^2$
$(x+9y)(x-7y)$

20. $x^2 + 8xy - 33y^2$
$(x+11y)(x-3y)$

©1995 Kelley Wingate Publications, Inc.   42   KW 1010

Worksheet 43

Name_____ *Factoring*

Factoring Trinomials of the form ax² + bx + c

$$3x^2 - 9x - 12 = 3(x^2-3x-4) = 3(x-4)(x+1)$$

Factor.

1. $5x^2 - 10x - 15$
$5(x-3)(x+1)$

2. $6x^2 - 15x - 21$
$3(x+1)(2x-7)$

3. $3x^2 - 10x + 7$
$(3x-7)(x-1)$

4. $2x^2 - 11x - 21$
$(2x+3)(x-7)$

5. $4x^2 + 2x - 20$
$2(2x+5)(x-2)$

6. $3x^2 - 5x - 12$
$(3x+4)(x-3)$

7. $7x^2 - 26x - 8$
$(7x+2)(x-4)$

8. $12x^2 - 6x - 18$
$6(2x-3)(x+1)$

9. $6x^2 - 13x + 6$
$(3x-2)(2x-3)$

10. $2x^2 + 9x + 10$
$(2x+5)(x+2)$

11. $3x^2 - 4x - 32$
$(3x+8)(x-4)$

12. $4x^2 - 16x + 15$
$(2x-3)(2x-5)$

13. $4x^2 + 7x - 15$
$(4x-5)(x+3)$

14. $6a^2 - 21a + 15$
$3(a-1)(2a-5)$

15. $11x^2 + 122x + 11$
$(11x+1)(x+11)$

16. $3x^2 - 20x - 7$
$(3x+1)(x-7)$

17. $2y^2 - 17y + 35$
$(2y-7)(y-5)$

18. $4x^2 - 16x + 15$
$(2x-3)(2x-5)$

19. $6x^2 + 25x + 25$
$(3x+5)(2x+5)$

20. $7c^2 - 16c + 9$
$(7c-9)(c-1)$

©1995 Kelley Wingate Publications, Inc.   43   KW 1010

Worksheet 44

Name_____ *Factoring*

Factoring Trinomials of the form ax² + bx + c

$$3x^2 - 9x - 12 = (3x + 3)(x - 4)$$

Factor.

1. $7x^2 + 17x + 6$
$(7x+3)(x+2)$

2. $5x^2 - 18x + 16$
$(5x-8)(x-2)$

3. $12x^2 - 40x + 25$
$(6x-5)(2x-5)$

4. $6x^2 - 21x - 12$
$(6x+3)(x-4)$

5. $4x^2 + 7x - 15$
$(4x-5)(x+3)$

6. $11x^2 - 122x + 11$
$(11x-1)(x-11)$

7. $9x^2 - 9x - 28$
$(3x+4)(3x-7)$

8. $2x^2 + 13x + 6$
$(2x+1)(x+6)$

9. $6x^2 + 5x - 6$
$(2x+3)(3x-2)$

10. $2x^2 - 11x - 40$
$(2x+5)(x-8)$

11. $10x^2 - 28x - 6$
$(10x+2)(x-3)$

12. $4x^2 - x - 5$
$(4x-5)(x+1)$

13. $12x^2 + 16x - 3$
$(6x-1)(2x+3)$

14. $2x^2 + 17x + 35$
$(2x+7)(x+5)$

15. $15x^2 - 29x - 14$
$(5x+2)(3x-7)$

16. $4x^2 - 7x - 15$
$(4x+5)(x-3)$

17. $14x^2 - 11x + 2$
$(7x-2)(2x-1)$

18. $2x^2 + 7x + 3$
$(2x+1)(x+3)$

19. $4x^2 - 15x + 9$
$(4x-3)(x-3)$

20. $6x^2 + x - 12$
$(3x-4)(2x+3)$

©1995 Kelley Wingate Publications, Inc.   44   KW 1010

Answer Key

Factoring Trinomials That are Quadratic in Form

$$x^4 - x^2 - 12 = (x^2)^2 - (x^2) - 12 = (x^2 - 4)(x^2 + 3) = (x + 2)(x - 2)(x^2 + 3) = (x^2 - 4)(x^2 + 3)$$

Factor.

1. $x^2y^2 - 8xy + 15$
$(xy-5)(xy-3)$

2. $x^2y^2 - 18xy + 32$
$(xy-16)(xy-2)$

3. $x^2y^2 + 10xy + 24$
$(xy+6)(xy+4)$

4. $x^4 - 8x^2 + 15$
$(x^2-5)(x^2-3)$

5. $y^4 - 4y^2 - 12$
$(y^2-6)(y^2+2)$

6. $x^4y^4 - 19x^2y^2 + 34$
$(x^2y^2-17)(x^2y^2-2)$

7. $2x^2 - 13x + 15$
$(2x-3)(x-5)$

8. $3x^4 + 20x^2 + 33$
$(3x^2+11)(x^2+3)$

9. $2x^2 - 5x - 12$
$(2x+3)(x-4)$

10. $8x^4 - 23x^2 - 3$
$(8x^2+1)(x^2-3)$

11. $y^4 + 6y^2 - 16$
$(y^2+8)(y^2-2)$

12. $x^4y^4 - 8x^2y^2 + 12$
$(x^2y^2-2)(x^2y^2-6)$

13. $6x^2y^2 - 29xy + 23$
$(6xy-23)(xy+1)(xy-1)$

14. $7x^4 + 17x^2 + 6$
$(7x^2+3)(x^2+2)$

15. $x^4y^4 - x^2y^2 - 12$
$(x^2y^2+3)(x^2y^2-4)$

16. $2x^4y^4 - 7x^2y^2 + 30$
$(2x^2y^2+5)(2x^2y^2-6)$

17. $6a^4 + 25a^2b^2 - 25$
$(6a^3b^3-5)(a^3b^3+5)$

18. $4x^4y^4 - 2x^2y^2 - 56$
$(2x^2y^2+7)(2x^2y^2-8)$

19. $2x^4 + 13x^2 - 15$
$(2x^2+15)(x+1)(x-1)$

20. $2x^4 + 16x^2 + 3$
$2(x^2+5)(x^2+3)$

Factoring: Difference of Two Squares

Rule: $a^2 - b^2 = (a + b)(a - b)$ **Example:** $x^2 - 36 = (x + 6)(x - 6)$

Factor.

1. $x^2 - 16$
$(x+4)(x-4)$

2. $y^2 - 49$
$(y+7)(y-7)$

3. $4x^2 - 1$
$(2x+1)(2x-1)$

4. $81x^2 - 4$
$(9x+2)(9x-2)$

5. $16x^2 - 121$
$(4x+11)(4x-11)$

6. $49x^2 - 36$
$(7x+6)(7x-6)$

7. $1 - 9x^2$
$(1+3x)(1-3x)$

8. $16 - 81x^2$
$(4+9x)(4-9x)$

9. $x^2y^2 - 100$
$(xy+10)(xy-10)$

10. $x^2y^2 - 25$
$(xy+5)(xy-5)$

11. $x^2 - 4$
$(x+2)(x-2)$

12. $25 - x^2y^2$
$(5+xy)(5-xy)$

13. $64 - x^2y^2$
$(8+xy)(8-xy)$

14. $4x^2 - y^2$
$(2x+y)(2x-y)$

15. $49x^2 - 16y^4$
$(7x+4y^2)(7x-4y^2)$

16. $a^2 - 1$
$(a+1)(a-1)$

17. $c^2 - 16$
$(c+4)(c-4)$

18. $a^2 - 36$
$(a+6)(a-6)$

19. $b^2 - 9$
$(b+3)(b-3)$

20. $y^2 - 81$
$(y+9)(y-9)$

Factoring Perfect Square Trinomials

Rule: $a^2 + 2ab + b^2 = (a + b)^2$ $a^2 - 2ab + b^2 = (a - b)^2$
Example: $4x^2 + 4x + 1 = (2x + 1)^2$ $x^2 - 4x + 4 = (x + 2)^2$

Factor.

1. $x^2 - 14x + 49$
$(x-7)^2$

2. $b^2 - 18b + 81$
$(b-9)^2$

3. $x^2 - 12x + 36$
$(x-6)^2$

4. $c^2 - 6c + 9$
$(c-3)^2$

5. $x^2 - 2x + 1$
$(x-1)^2$

6. $x^2 + 14x + 49$
$(x+7)^2$

7. $16x^2 - 40x + 25$
$(4x-5)^2$

8. $49x^2 + 28x + 4$
$(7x+2)^2$

9. $4x^2 + 4x + 1$
$(2x+1)^2$

10. $9x^2 + 12x + 4$
$(3x+2)^2$

11. $x^2 + 8x + 16$
$(x+4)^2$

12. $x^2 - 10x + 25$
$(x-5)^2$

13. $a^2 + 12ab + 36b^2$
$(a + 6b)^2$

14. $x^2 - 14x + 49$
$(x-7)^2$

15. $9x^2 - 6x + 1$
$(3x-1)^2$

16. $x^2 - 16x + 64$
$(x-8)^2$

17. $y^2 - 24y + 144$
$(y-12)^2$

18. $25a^2 - 40ab + 16b^2$
$(5a-4b)^2$

19. $x^2 - 4x + 4$
$(x-2)^2$

20. $c^2 - 20c + 100$
$(c-10)^2$

Factoring the Sum or the Difference of Two Cubes

Rule: $x^3 + y^3 = (x + y)(x^2 - xy + y^2)$ $x^3 - y^3 = (x - y)(x^2 + xy + y^2)$
Example: $x^3 + 8 = (x + 2)(x^2 - 2x + 4)$ $x^3 - 8 = (x - 2)(x^2 + 2x + 4)$

Factor.

1. $x^3 - 1000$
$(x-10)(x^2+10x + 100)$

2. $8x^3 - 1$
$(2x-1)(4x^2+2x+1)$

3. $x^3 - y^3$
$(x-y)(x^2+xy + y^2)$

4. $x^3 + y^3$
$(x+y)(x^2-xy+y^2)$

5. $64x^3 + 1$
$(4x+1)(16x^2-4x+1)$

6. $27x^3 - 8y^3$
$(3x-2y)(9x^2+6xy+4y^2)$

7. $x^3y^3 + 64$
$(xy+4)(x^2y^2-4xy+16)$

8. $x^3 + 125$
$(x+5)(x^2-5x+25)$

9. $64x^3 + 27$
$(4x+3)(16x^2-12x+9)$

10. $x^3 - 8y^3$
$(x-2y)(x^2+2xy+4y^2)$

11. $27x^3 + y^3$
$(3x+y)(9x^2-3xy+y^2)$

12. $1 - 125y^3$
$(1-5y)(1+5y+25y^2)$

13. $64x^3 + 27y^3$
$(4x+3y)(16x^2-12xy+9y^2)$

14. $8x^3 + 27$
$(2x+3)(4x^2-6x+9)$

15. $64x^3 - y^3$
$(4x-y)(16x^2+4xy+y^2)$

16. $x^3 - 27$
$(x-3)(x^2+3x+9)$

17. $8x^3 - 216$
$(2x-6)(4x^2+12x+36)$

18. $125a^3 - 8b^3$
$(5a-2b)(25a^2+10ab+4b^2)$

19. $27x^3 - 64$
$(3x-4)(9x^2+12x+16)$

20. $27x^3 - 1$
$(3x-1)(9x^2+3x+1)$

Answer Key

Solving Equations by Factoring

The Multiplication Property of Zero: The product of a number and zero is zero.
The Principle of Zero Products states that if the product of two factors is zero,
then at least one of the factors must be zero. This principle is used in solving
equations.
Solve: $(x - 5)(x - 6) = 0$ If $(x - 5)(x - 6) = 0$, then $(x - 5) = 0$ or $(x - 6) = 0$.
$x - 5 = 0$ $x - 6 = 0$
$x = 5$ $x = 6$
The solutions are 5 and 6.

$(x - 5)(x - 6) = 0$	$(x - 5)(x - 6) = 0$
$(5 - 5)(5 - 6)$ | 0	$(6 - 5)(6 - 6)$ | 0
$0(-1)$ | 0	$0(-1)$ | 0
$0 = 0$	$0 = 0$

1. $(y + 5)(y + 6) = 0$
$-5, -6$

2. $x(x + 7) = 0$
$0, -7$

3. $(2x + 4)(x + 7) = 0$
$-2, -7$

4. $(y - 4)(y - 8) = 0$
$4, 8$

5. $z^2 - 4 = 0$
$2, -2$

6. $(4y - 1)(y + 2) = 0$
$\frac{1}{4}, -2$

7. $y(y - 12) = 0$
$0, 12$

8. $4y(3y - 2) = 0$
$0, \frac{2}{3}$

9. $b^2 - 49 = 0$ $7, -7$

10. $m^2 - 100 = 0$
$10, -10$

11. $2x^2 - 6x = x - 3$
$\frac{1}{2}, 3$

12. $z^2 - 1 = 0$
$1, -1$

13. $(2y - 1)(y - 2) = 0$
$\frac{1}{2}, 2$

14. $x^2 - 5x + 6 = 0$
$3, 2$

15. $8b^2 - 32 = 0$
$2, -2$

16. $x^2 - x - 2 = 0$
$2, -1$

17. $10x^2 - 10x = 0$
$0, 1$

18. $x^2 - 3x - 28 = 0$ $7, -4$

Problem Solving

The length of a rectangle is 5 in. longer than the width. The area of
the rectangle is 50 in.² Find the length and width of the rectangle.
Width of rectangle: w
Length of rectangle: w + 5

$A = LW$
$50 = (w + 5)(w)$
$50 = w^2 + 5w$
$0 = w^2 + 5w - 50$
$0 = (w + 10)(w - 5)$
$w + 10 = 0$ $w - 5 = 0$

Since the width cannot be a negative
number the answer is 5.
$w + 5 = 5 + 5 = 10$
The length is 10 and the width is 5.

For each word problem, write an equation and solve it.

1. The sum of a number and its square is 30. Find the numbers.
Equation $x^2 + x = 30$
Solution $-6, 5$

2. The sum of twice a number and its square is 143. Find the numbers.
Equation $2x + x^2 = 143$
Solution $-13, 11$

3. The sum of a number and its square is 20. Find the numbers.
Equation $x^2 + x = 20$
Solution $-5, 4$

4. For what numbers is the sum of a number and its square equal to 42?
Equation $x^2 + x = 42$
Solution $-7, 6$

5. The square of a number is 70 more than 3 times the number. Find the numbers.
Equation $x^2 = 70 + 3x$
Solution $10, -7$

6. The square of a number is 35 more than twice the number. Find the numbers.
Equation $x^2 = 2x + 35$
Solution $7, -5$

7. The sum of a number and its square is 72. Find the numbers.
Equation $x^2 + x = 72$
Solution $-9, 8$

Problem Solving

The length of a rectangle is 5 in. longer than the width. The area
of the rectangle is 50 in.² Find the length and width of the
rectangle.
Width of rectangle: w
Length of rectangle: w + 5
$A = LW$
$50 = (w + 5)(w)$
$50 = w^2 + 5w$
$0 = w^2 + 5w - 50$
$0 = (w + 10)(w - 5)$
$w + 10 = 0$ $w - 5 = 0$

Since the width cannot be a negative
number the answer is 5.
$w + 5 = 5 + 5 = 10$
The length is 10 and the width is 5.

For each word problem, write an equation and solve it.

1. The area of a rectangle is 72 m². Its length is twice its width. Find the length
and width of the rectangle.
Equation $(2w)(w) = 72$
Solution $L = 12 m$ $W = 6 m$

2. The width of a rectangle is three more than twice its length. The
area of the rectangle is 44in². Find the dimensions of the rectangle
Equation $L(3 + 2L) = 44$
Solution $L = 4 in$ $W = 11 in$

3. The area of a square is 144m². Find the length of the sides of the
square.
Equation $s^2 = 144$
Solution $L = 12 m$

4. The area of a rectangle is 27 cm². Its width is three times its length.
Find the length and width of the rectangle.
Equation $(3L)(L) = 27$
Solution $L = 3 cm$ $W = 9 cm$

5. the length of a rectangle is 4 more than twice its width. The area of
the rectangle is 96ft². Find its dimensions.
Equation $x(2x + 4) = 96$
Solution $L = 16 ft$ $W = 6 ft$

Dividing Monomials

$$\frac{25x^4y^4}{5x^2y^2} = \frac{25}{5} \cdot y^{4-2} \cdot y^{4-2} = \frac{5x^2}{y^2}$$

Simplify.

1. $\frac{x^3}{x^5} = \frac{1}{x^2}$

2. $\frac{a^4b^2}{2a^3} = \frac{a^2b^2}{2}$

3. $\frac{12x^2y^4}{3x^2y^3} = 4y$

4. $\frac{10a^6b^6}{40a^2b^3} = \frac{a^4b^4}{4}$

5. $\frac{14c^2d^2}{28cd} = \frac{cd}{2}$

6. $\frac{18a^3b^3}{36a^2b^2} = \frac{a^2b}{2}$

7. $\frac{13m^6n^7}{26m^2n^5} = \frac{m^4n^2}{2}$

8. $\frac{35x^4y^{10}z^3}{15x^4y^2z^1} = \frac{7y^2z^2}{3}$

9. $\frac{5x^2y^2z^3}{5x^2yz} = xyz$

10. $\frac{72x^4y^3z^3}{9x^2yz} = 8xy^4z^3$

11. $\frac{6x^5y^3z^3}{12x^2y^2z^2} = \frac{x^3yz}{2}$

12. $\frac{9x^4y^2z^3}{27x^2yz} = \frac{x^4y^2z^4}{3}$

13. $\frac{18a^3b^3c^4}{36a^2bc^3} = \frac{a^2bc^4}{2}$

14. $\frac{33x^4y^2}{11x^3yz} = \frac{3y}{z}$

Simplifying Rational Expressions

Name_____ *Rational Expressions*

$$\frac{a^2+7a+5}{a}=\frac{a^2}{a}+\frac{7a}{a}+\frac{5}{a}$$
$$=a+7+\frac{5}{a}$$

Simplify.

1. $\frac{x^3+2x}{x}=$ x^2+2

2. $\frac{18x+36}{9}=$ $2x+4$

3. $\frac{8y^2+12y^3}{6y}=$ $\frac{4y}{3}+2y^2$

4. $\frac{10a^5b^8+8a^3b^5}{ab}=$ $10a^5b^7+8a^2b^4$

5. $\frac{3cd^2+6c^2d}{3cd}=$ $d+2c$

6. $\frac{18x^4-9x^3-3x}{-3}=$ $-6x^3+3x^2+x$

7. $\frac{m^5n^7+m-n}{m^3n}=$ $m^4n^6+\frac{1}{mn}-\frac{1}{m^2}$

8. $\frac{12a^3-9a^2-3a}{-3a}=$ $-4a^2+3a+1$

9. $\frac{9x^4-3x^2-12xy^3}{3xy^3}=$ $\frac{3x^3}{y^3}-\frac{x}{y^3}-4$

10. $\frac{2x^2y^2-2x^3y^3-4xy^2}{2x^2y^2}=$ $\frac{x}{y}-\frac{9x}{y^2}-\frac{2}{x}$

11. $\frac{12a^2-2a+12}{2a}=$ $6a-1+\frac{6}{a}$

12. $\frac{9x^4+3x+3}{3x}=$ $3x^7+1+\frac{1}{x}$

13. $\frac{x^2y^3+x-y}{x^2y}=$ $y^2+\frac{1}{x^2}y-\frac{1}{x^3}$

14. $\frac{3x^4y^5+12x^2y^3-18x^2}{x^2y}=$ $3x^2y^4+12y^2-\frac{18}{y}$

Dividing Polynomials

Name_____ *Rational Expressions*

Simplify: $(x^2 + 6x + 5) \div (x + 1)$

$$\begin{array}{r} x + 5 \\ x+1\overline{)\ x^2 + 6x + 5} \\ \underline{x^2 + 1x} \\ 5x + 5 \\ \underline{5x + 5} \\ 0 \end{array}$$

Divide by using long division.

1. $(x^2 + 2x - 35) \div (x + 7) =$ $(x-5)$

2. $(x^2 - 10x + 24) \div (x - 4)$ $(x-6)$

3. $(x^2 + 4x + 3) \div (x + 1) =$ $(x+3)$

4. $(x^2 + 5x + 6) \div (x + 3) =$ $(x+2)$

5. $(x^2 + 7x + 10) \div (x + 2) =$ $(x+5)$

6. $(x^2 + 4x - 21) \div (x - 3) =$ $(x+7)$

7. $(x^2 + 9x + 8) \div (x + 8) =$ $(x+1)$

8. $(x^2 - 6x + 9) \div (x - 3) =$ $(x-3)$

9. $(x^2 - x - 42) \div (x + 6) =$ $(x-7)$

10. $(x^2 - 3x - 40) \div (x + 5) =$ $(x-8)$

Dividing Polynomials

Name_____ *Rational Expressions*

Simplify: $\frac{(4x^2 + 4x - 3)}{(2x + 3)}$

$$\begin{array}{r} 2x - 1 \\ 2x+3\overline{)\ 4x^2 + 4x - 3} \\ \underline{4x^2 + 6x} \\ -2x - 3 \\ \underline{-2x - 3} \\ 0 \end{array}$$

Divide by using long division.

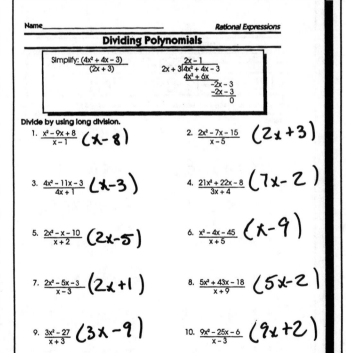

1. $\frac{x^2 - 9x + 8}{x - 1}$ $(x-8)$

2. $\frac{2x^2 - 7x - 15}{x - 5}$ $(2x+3)$

3. $\frac{4x^2 - 11x - 3}{4x + 1}$ $(x-3)$

4. $\frac{21x^2 + 22x - 8}{3x + 4}$ $(7x-2)$

5. $\frac{2x^2 - x - 10}{x + 2}$ $(2x-5)$

6. $\frac{x^2 - 4x - 45}{x + 5}$ $(x-9)$

7. $\frac{2x^2 - 5x - 3}{x - 3}$ $(2x+1)$

8. $\frac{5x^2 + 43x - 18}{x + 9}$ $(5x-2)$

9. $\frac{3x^2 - 27}{x + 3}$ $(3x-9)$

10. $\frac{9x^2 - 25x - 6}{x - 3}$ $(9x+2)$

Dividing Polynomials by Synthetic Division

Name_____ *Rational Expressions*

Simplify: $(2x^3 + 3x^2 - 4x + 8) \div (x + 3)$

$$\begin{array}{r} -3\,|\begin{array}{rrrr} 2 & 3 & -4 & 8 \\ & -6 & 9 & -15 \\ \hline 2 & -3 & 5 & -7 \end{array} \end{array}$$

$$= 2x^2 - 3x + 5 - \frac{7}{x + 3}$$

Divide by using synthetic division.

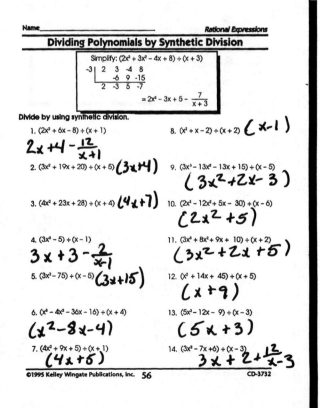

1. $(2x^2 + 6x - 8) \div (x + 1)$ $2x+4-\frac{12}{x+1}$

2. $(3x^2 + 19x + 20) \div (x + 5)$ $(3x+4)$

3. $(4x^2 + 23x + 28) \div (x + 4)$ $(4x+7)$

4. $(3x^2 - 5) \div (x - 1)$ $3x+3-\frac{2}{x-1}$

5. $(3x^2 - 75) \div (x - 5)$ $(3x+15)$

6. $(x^2 - 4x - 36x - 16) \div (x + 4)$ (x^2-8x-4)

7. $(4x^2 + 9x + 5) \div (x + 1)$ $(4x+5)$

8. $(x^2 + x - 2) \div (x + 2)$ $(x-1)$

9. $(3x^3 - 13x^2 - 13x + 15) \div (x - 5)$ $(3x^2+2x-3)$

10. $(2x^3 - 12x^2 + 5x - 30) \div (x - 6)$ $(2x^2+5)$

11. $(3x^3 + 8x^2 + 9x + 10) \div (x + 2)$ $(3x^2+2x+5)$

12. $(x^2 + 14x + 45) \div (x + 5)$ $(x+9)$

13. $(5x^2 - 12x - 9) \div (x - 3)$ $(5x+3)$

14. $(3x^2 - 7x + 6) \div (x - 3)$ $3x+2+\frac{12}{x-3}$

Answer Key

Answer Key

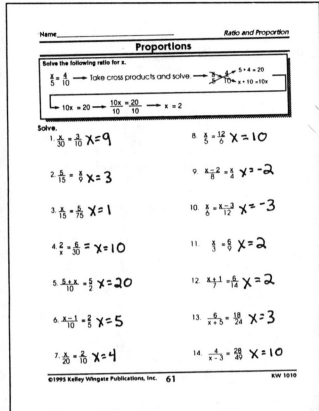

Proportions

Solve the following ratio for x.

$\frac{x}{5} = \frac{4}{10}$ → Take cross products and solve. → $\frac{x}{5} \times \frac{4}{10}$ $5 \cdot 4 = 20$ $x \cdot 10 = 10x$

→ $10x = 20$ → $\frac{10x}{10} = \frac{20}{10}$ → $x = 2$

Solve.

1. $\frac{x}{30} = \frac{3}{10}$ $x = 9$

2. $\frac{5}{15} = \frac{x}{9}$ $x = 3$

3. $\frac{x}{15} = \frac{5}{75}$ $x = 1$

4. $\frac{2}{x} = \frac{6}{30}$ $x = 10$

5. $\frac{5+x}{10} = \frac{5}{2}$ $x = 20$

6. $\frac{x-1}{10} = \frac{2}{5}$ $x = 5$

7. $\frac{x}{20} = \frac{2}{10}$ $x = 4$

8. $\frac{x}{5} = \frac{12}{6}$ $x = 10$

9. $\frac{x-2}{8} = \frac{x}{4}$ $x = -2$

10. $\frac{x}{6} = \frac{x-3}{12}$ $x = -3$

11. $\frac{x}{3} = \frac{6}{9}$ $x = 2$

12. $\frac{x+1}{7} = \frac{6}{14}$ $x = 2$

13. $\frac{6}{x+5} = \frac{18}{24}$ $x = 3$

14. $\frac{4}{x-3} = \frac{28}{49}$ $x = 10$

©1995 Kelley Wingate Publications, Inc.   61   KW 1010

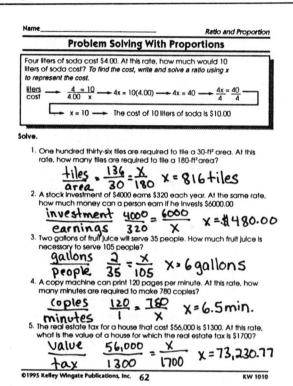

Problem Solving With Proportions

Four liters of soda cost $4.00. At this rate, how much would 10 liters of soda cost? *To find the cost, write and solve a ratio using x to represent the cost.*

$\frac{liters}{cost}$ → $\frac{4}{4.00} = \frac{10}{x}$ → $4x = 10(4.00)$ → $4x = 40$ → $\frac{4x}{4} = \frac{40}{4}$

→ $x = 10$ → The cost of 10 liters of soda is $10.00

Solve.

1. One hundred thirty-six tiles are required to tile a 30-ft² area. At this rate, how many tiles are required to tile a 180-ft² area?

$\frac{tiles}{area} = \frac{136}{30} = \frac{x}{180}$ $x = 816$ tiles

2. A stock investment of $4000 earns $320 each year. At the same rate, how much money can a person earn if he invests $6000.00?

$\frac{investment}{earnings}$ $\frac{4000}{320} = \frac{6000}{x}$ $x = \$480.00$

3. Two gallons of fruit juice will serve 35 people. How much fruit juice is necessary to serve 105 people?

$\frac{gallons}{people}$ $\frac{2}{35} = \frac{x}{105}$ $x = 6$ gallons

4. A copy machine can print 120 pages per minute. At this rate, how many minutes are required to make 780 copies?

$\frac{copies}{minutes}$ $\frac{120}{1} = \frac{780}{x}$ $x = 6.5$ min.

5. The real estate tax for a house that cost $56,000 is $1300. At this rate, what is the value of a house for which the real estate tax is $1700?

$\frac{value}{tax}$ $\frac{56,000}{1300} = \frac{x}{1700}$ $x = 73,230.77$

©1995 Kelley Wingate Publications, Inc.   62   KW 1010

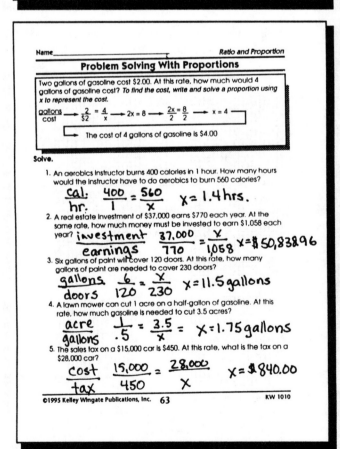

Problem Solving With Proportions

Two gallons of gasoline cost $2.00. At this rate, how much would 4 gallons of gasoline cost? *To find the cost, write and solve a proportion using x to represent the cost.*

$\frac{gallons}{cost}$ → $\frac{2}{\$2} = \frac{4}{x}$ → $2x = 8$ → $\frac{2x}{2} = \frac{8}{2}$ → $x = 4$

→ The cost of 4 gallons of gasoline is $4.00

Solve.

1. An aerobics instructor burns 400 calories in 1 hour. How many hours would the instructor have to do aerobics to burn 560 calories?

$\frac{cal.}{hr.}$ $\frac{400}{1} = \frac{560}{x}$ $x = 1.4$ hrs.

2. A real estate investment of $37,000 earns $770 each year. At the same rate, how much money must be invested to earn $1,058 each year?

$\frac{investment}{earnings}$ $\frac{37,000}{770} = \frac{x}{1,058}$ $x = \$50,832.96$

3. Six gallons of paint will cover 120 doors. At this rate, how many gallons of paint are needed to cover 230 doors?

$\frac{gallons}{doors}$ $\frac{6}{120} = \frac{x}{230}$ $x = 11.5$ gallons

4. A lawn mower can cut 1 acre on a half-gallon of gasoline. At this rate, how much gasoline is needed to cut 3.5 acres?

$\frac{acre}{gallons}$ $\frac{1}{.5} = \frac{3.5}{x}$ $x = 1.75$ gallons

5. The sales tax on a $15,000 car is $450. At this rate, what is the tax on a $28,000 car?

$\frac{cost}{tax}$ $\frac{15,000}{450} = \frac{28,000}{x}$ $x = \$840.00$

©1995 Kelley Wingate Publications, Inc.   63   KW 1010

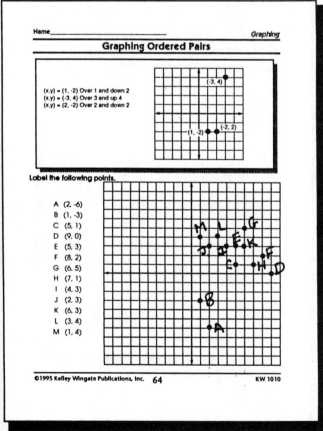

Graphing Ordered Pairs

(x,y) = (1, -2) Over 1 and down 2
(x,y) = (-3, 4) Over 3 and up 4
(x,y) = (2, -2) Over 2 and down 2

Label the following points.

A (2, -6)
B (1, -3)
C (5, 1)
D (9, 0)
E (5, 3)
F (8, 2)
G (6, 5)
H (7, 1)
I (4, 3)
J (2, 3)
K (6, 3)
L (3, 4)
M (1, 4)

©1995 Kelley Wingate Publications, Inc.   64   KW 1010

Answer Key

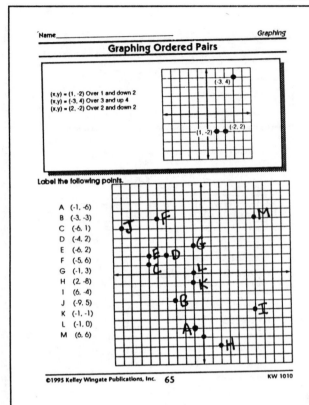

Graphing Ordered Pairs

(x,y) = (1, -2) Over 1 and down 2
(x,y) = (-3, 4) Over 3 and up 4
(x,y) = (2, -2) Over 2 and down 2

Label the following points.

A (-1, -6)
B (-3, -3)
C (-6, 1)
D (-4, 2)
E (-6, 2)
F (-5, 6)
G (-1, 3)
H (2, -8)
I (6, -4)
J (-9, 5)
K (-1, -1)
L (-1, 0)
M (6, 6)

©1995 Kelley Wingate Publications, Inc.   65   KW 1010

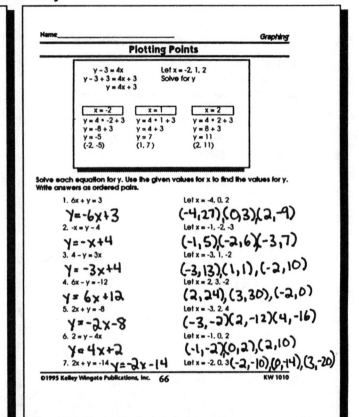

Plotting Points

y − 3 = 4x   Let x = -2, 1, 2
y − 3 + 3 = 4x + 3   Solve for y
y = 4x + 3

x = -2	x = 1	x = 2
y = 4 • -2 + 3	y = 4 • 1 + 3	y = 4 • 2 + 3
y = -8 + 3	y = 4 + 3	y = 8 + 3
y = -5	y = 7	y = 11
(-2, -5)	(1, 7)	(2, 11)

Solve each equation for y. Use the given values for x to find the values for y.
Write answers as ordered pairs.

1. 6x + y = 3   Let x = -4, 0, 2
$y = -6x + 3$ (-4, 27), (0, 3), (2, -9)

2. -x = y − 4   Let x = -1, -2, -3
$y = -x + 4$ (-1, 5), (-2, 6), (-3, 7)

3. 4 − y = 3x   Let x = -3, 1, -2
$y = -3x + 4$ (-3, 13), (1, 1), (-2, 10)

4. 6x − y = -12   Let x = 2, 3, -2
$y = 6x + 12$ (2, 24), (3, 30), (-2, 0)

5. 2x + y = -8   Let x = -3, 2, 4
$y = -2x - 8$ (-3, -2), (2, -12), (4, -16)

6. 2 = y − 4x   Let x = -1, 0, 2
$y = 4x + 2$ (-1, -2), (0, 2), (2, 10)

7. 2x + y = -14 $y = -2x - 14$ Let x = -2, 0, 3   (-2, -10), (0, -14), (3, -20)

©1995 Kelley Wingate Publications, Inc.   66   KW 1010

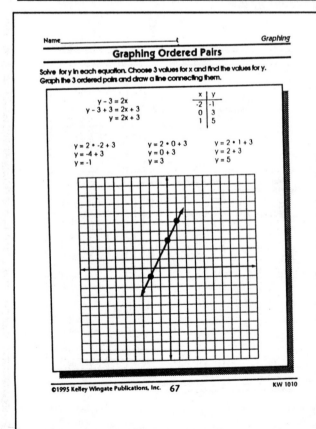

Graphing Ordered Pairs

Solve for y in each equation. Choose 3 values for x and find the values for y.
Graph the 3 ordered pairs and draw a line connecting them.

y − 3 = 2x
y − 3 + 3 = 2x + 3
y = 2x + 3

x	y
-2	-1
0	3
1	5

y = 2 • -2 + 3   y = 2 • 0 + 3   y = 2 • 1 + 3
y = -4 + 3   y = 0 + 3   y = 2 + 3
y = -1   y = 3   y = 5

©1995 Kelley Wingate Publications, Inc.   67   KW 1010

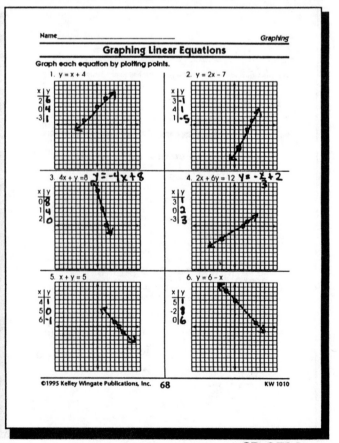

Graphing Linear Equations

Graph each equation by plotting points.

1. y = x + 4

x	y
2	6
0	4
-3	1

2. y = 2x − 7

x	y
3	-1
4	1
1	-5

3. 4x + y = 8   y = -4x + 8

x	y
0	8
1	4
2	0

4. 2x + 6y = 12 $y = -\frac{x}{3} + 2$

x	y
3	1
0	2
-3	3

5. x + y = 5

x	y
4	1
5	0
6	-1

6. y = 6 − x

x	y
5	1
-2	8
0	6

©1995 Kelley Wingate Publications, Inc.   68   KW 1010

Answer Key

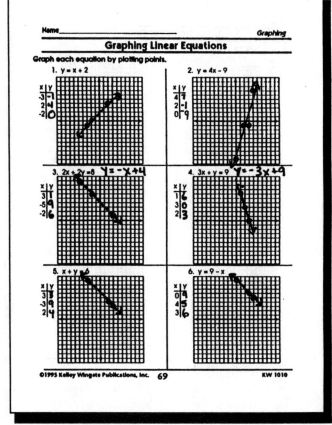

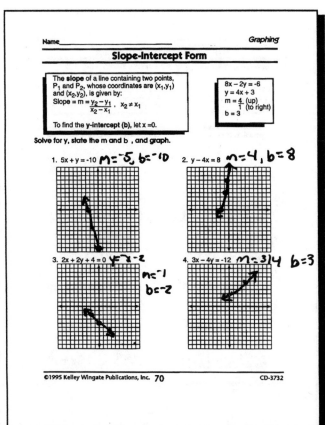

Name_____   *Graphing*

Slope-Intercept Form

The **slope** of a line containing two points, P_1 and P_2, whose coordinates are (x_1, y_1) and (x_2, y_2), is given by:

Slope = $m = \dfrac{y_2 - y_1}{x_2 - x_1}$, $x_2 \neq x_1$

To find the y-intercept (b), let x = 0.

8x - 2y = -6
y = 4x + 3
m = $\frac{4}{1}$ (up) (to right)
b = 3

Solve for y, state the m and b, and graph.

1. 5x + y = -10   m = -5, b = -10

2. y - 4x = 8   m = 4, b = 8

3. 2x + 2y + 4 = 0   y = -x - 2   m = -1   b = -2

4. 3x - 4y = -12   m = 3/4   b = 3

©1995 Kelley Wingate Publications, Inc.   70   CD-3732

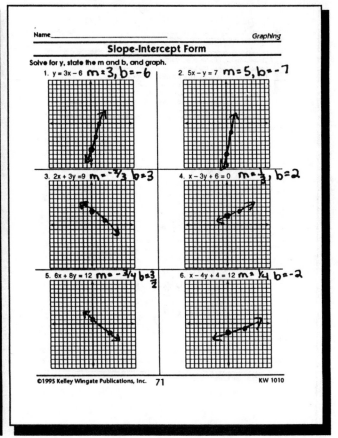

Name_____   *Graphing*

Slope-Intercept Form

Solve for y, state the m and b, and graph.

1. y = 3x - 6   m = 3, b = -6

2. 5x - y = 7   m = 5, b = -7

3. 2x + 3y = 9   m = -2/3 b = 3

4. x - 3y + 6 = 0   m = 3, b = 2

5. 6x + 8y = 12   m = -3/4 b = 3/2

6. x - 4y + 4 = 12   m = 1/4 b = -2

©1995 Kelley Wingate Publications, Inc.   71   KW 1010

Answer Key

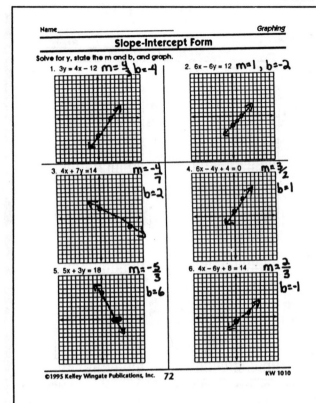

Name_____ *Graphing*

Slope-Intercept Form

Solve for y, state the m and b, and graph.

1. $3y = 4x - 12$ $m = \frac{4}{3}$ $b = -4$

2. $6x - 6y = 12$ $m = 1$, $b = -2$

3. $4x + 7y = 14$ $m = -\frac{4}{7}$ $b = 2$

4. $6x - 4y + 4 = 0$ $m = \frac{3}{2}$ $b = 1$

5. $5x + 3y = 18$ $m = -\frac{5}{3}$ $b = 6$

6. $4x - 6y + 8 = 14$ $m = \frac{2}{3}$ $b = -1$

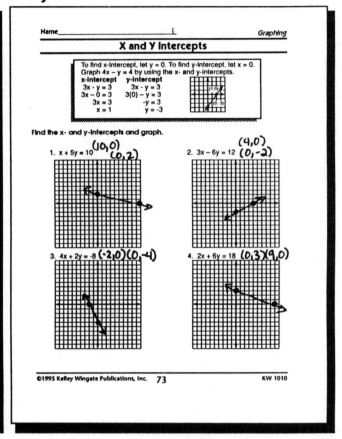

Name_____ i____ *Graphing*

X and Y Intercepts

To find x-intercept, let y = 0. To find y-intercept, let x = 0.
Graph $4x - y = 4$ by using the x- and y-intercepts.

x-intercept	y-intercept
$3x - y = 3$	$3x - y = 3$
$3x - 0 = 3$	$3(0) - y = 3$
$3x = 3$	$-y = 3$
$x = 1$	$y = -3$

Find the x- and y-intercepts and graph.

1. $x + 5y = 10$ $(10,0)$ $(0,2)$

2. $3x - 6y = 12$ $(4,0)$ $(0,-2)$

3. $4x + 2y = -8$ $(-2,0)(0,-4)$

4. $2x + 6y = 18$ $(0,3)(9,0)$

Name_____ *Graphing*

Writing an Equation of a Line

Slope-Intercept Form of a Straight Line
For all equations of the form y = mx + b, m is the slope of the line. The y-intercept is (0,b). This equation, y = mx + b, is the slope-intercept form of a straight line. When the equation is in the form Ax + By = C, solve the equation for y. Once you have solved for y, follow the same procedure used for an equation in the form y = mx + b.

Write each equation below in slope-intercept form.

1. $2y - x = 6$ $y = \frac{1}{2}x + 3$

2. $3y = 2x + 12$ $y = \frac{2}{3}x + 4$

3. $4y + 24 = 3x$ $y = \frac{3}{4}x - 6$

4. $4y - x = 32$ $y = \frac{1}{4}x + 8$

5. $-4x + y = 8$ $y = 4x + 8$

6. $y - x + 5 = 0$ $y = x - 5$

7. $-9x + 3y + 27 = 0$ $y = 3x - 9$

8. $y - 6 = 2x$ $y = 2x + 6$

Find the equation of a line in standard form using the slope-intercept form: y = mx + b

1. $m = 0$ $b = \frac{3}{5}$ $y = \frac{3}{5}$

2. $m = -5$ $b = \frac{3}{4}$ $y = -5x + \frac{3}{4}$

3. $m = \frac{3}{4}$ $b = \frac{2}{3}$ $y = \frac{3}{4}x + \frac{2}{3}$

4. $m = -\frac{9}{5}$ $b = -3$ $y = -\frac{9}{5}x - 3$

5. $m = \frac{1}{4}$ $b = \frac{1}{3}$

6. $m = \frac{3}{7}$ $b = \frac{2}{3}$

7. $m = \frac{3}{5}$ $b = \frac{1}{5}$

#5 $y = \frac{1}{4}x + \frac{1}{3}$

#6 $y = \frac{3}{7}x + \frac{2}{3}$

#7 $y = \frac{3}{5}x + \frac{1}{5}$

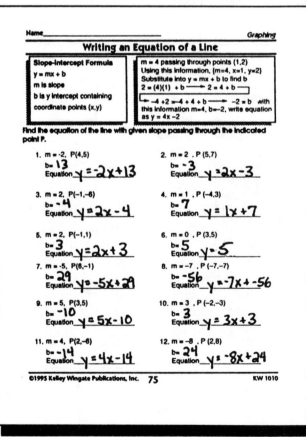

Name_____ *Graphing*

Writing an Equation of a Line

Slope-Intercept Formula
y = mx + b
m is slope
b is y intercept containing coordinate points (x,y)

m = 4 passing through points (1,2)
Using this information, (m=4, x=1, y=2)
Substitute into y = mx + b to find b
$2 = (4)(1) + b$ → $2 = 4 + b$
$-4 + 2 = -4 + 4 + b$ → $-2 = b$ with this information m=4, b=-2, write equation as y = 4x -2

Find the equation of the line with given slope passing through the indicated point P.

1. $m = -2$, $P(4,5)$
   $b = 13$
   Equation $y = -2x + 13$

2. $m = 2$, $P(5,7)$
   $b = -3$
   Equation $y = 2x - 3$

3. $m = 2$, $P(-1,-6)$
   $b = -4$
   Equation $y = 2x - 4$

4. $m = 1$, $P(-4,3)$
   $b = 7$
   Equation $y = 1x + 7$

5. $m = 2$, $P(-1,1)$
   $b = 3$
   Equation $y = 2x + 3$

6. $m = 0$, $P(3,5)$
   $b = 5$
   Equation $y = 5$

7. $m = -5$, $P(6,-1)$
   $b = 29$
   Equation $y = -5x + 29$

8. $m = -7$, $P(-7,-7)$
   $b = -56$
   Equation $y = -7x + -56$

9. $m = 5$, $P(3,5)$
   $b = -10$
   Equation $y = 5x - 10$

10. $m = 3$, $P(-2,-3)$
    $b = 3$
    Equation $y = 3x + 3$

11. $m = 4$, $P(2,-6)$
    $b = -14$
    Equation $y = 4x - 14$

12. $m = -8$, $P(2,8)$
    $b = 24$
    Equation $y = -8x + 24$

     CD-3732

Answer Key

Name_____
Graphing

Graphing Linear Inequalities

To Graph: y > 2x + 3

1. Graph line y = 2x + 3   m = $\frac{2}{1}$ b=3

2. If > or <, connect with dotted line.   3. If ≥ or ≤, connect with solid line

The coordinate plane is now divided into 2 regions.

4. Test any (x,y) on each side of line which divides plane into the 2 regions. Test (x,y) in original inequality.

y > 2x + 3
Test point A (-1, 4)
Is 4 > 2 (-1) + 3?
4 > -2 + 3
4 > 1 ⟶ true
(Shade this region)

y > 2x + 3
Test point b (0,0)
Is 0 > 2 (0) + 3?
0 > 0 + 3
0 > 3 ⟶ false
(Do not shade this region)

Graph the solution set.

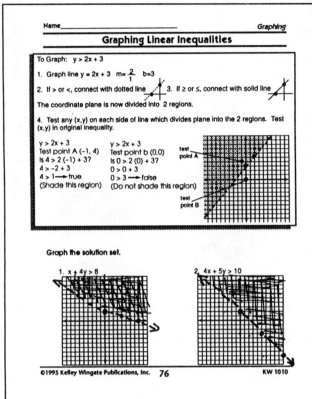

1. x + 4y > 8
2. 4x + 5y > 10

©1995 Kelley Wingate Publications, Inc. **76**   KW 1010

Name_____
Graphing

Graphing Linear Inequalities

Graph the solution set.

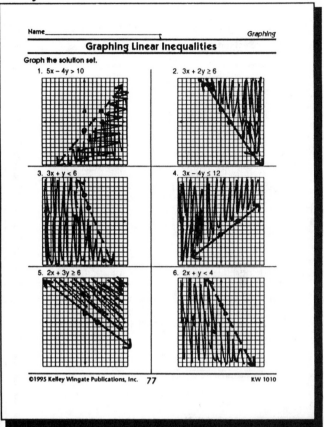

1. 5x – 4y > 10
2. 3x + 2y ≥ 6
3. 3x + y < 6
4. 3x – 4y ≤ 12
5. 2x + 3y ≥ 6
6. 2x + y < 4

©1995 Kelley Wingate Publications, Inc. **77**   KW 1010

Name_____
Graphing

Graphing Linear Inequalities

Graph the solution set.

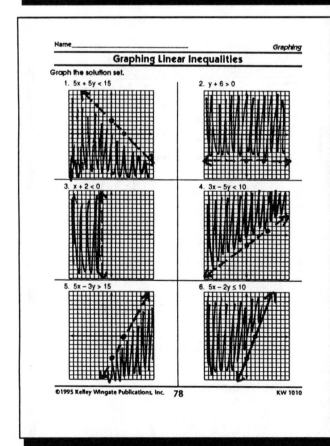

1. 5x + 5y < 15
2. y + 6 > 0
3. x + 2 < 0
4. 3x – 5y < 10
5. 5x – 3y > 15
6. 5x – 2y ≤ 10

©1995 Kelley Wingate Publications, Inc. **78**   KW 1010

Name_____
Graphing

Solving Systems of Linear Equations by Graphing

Two or more equations considered together is called a **system of equations**. The following example is a system of two linear equations in two variables.
x + 2y = 4
2x + y = –1
The graphs of these equations are straight lines.
An ordered pair that is a solution of each equation of the system is a **solution of the system of equations in two variables**.
The solution of a system of linear equations can be found by graphing the lines of the system. The solution of the system of equations is the point where the lines of the ordered pair intersects.
Solve by graphing:
x + 2y = 4
2x + y = –1
Graph each line and find the point of intersection.

The solution is (-2, 3) because the ordered pair lies on each line.

(-2, 3)

Solve by graphing.

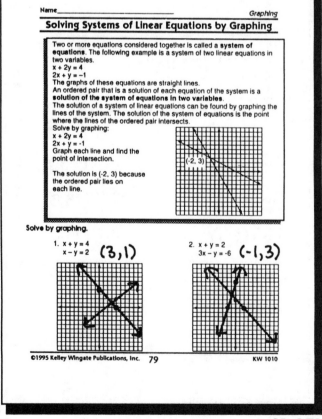

1. x + y = 4
    x – y = 2   (3,1)
2. x + y = 2
    3x – y = -6   (-1,3)

©1995 Kelley Wingate Publications, Inc. **79**   KW 1010

© 1996 Kelley Wingate Publications   123   CD-3732

Answer Key

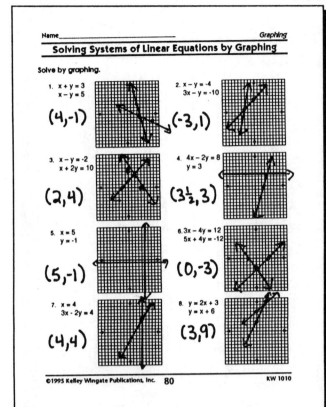

Solving Systems of Linear Equations by Graphing

Solve by graphing.

1. $x + y = 3$
   $x - y = 5$
   (4,-1)

2. $x - y = -4$
   $3x - y = -10$
   (-3,1)

3. $x - y = -2$
   $x + 2y = 10$
   (2,4)

4. $4x - 2y = 8$
   $y = 3$
   (3½,3)

5. $x = 5$
   $y = -1$
   (5,-1)

6. $3x - 4y = 12$
   $5x + 4y = -12$
   (0,-3)

7. $x = 4$
   $3x - 2y = 4$
   (4,4)

8. $y = 2x + 3$
   $y = x + 6$
   (3,9)

©1995 Kelley Wingate Publications, Inc.   80   KW 1010

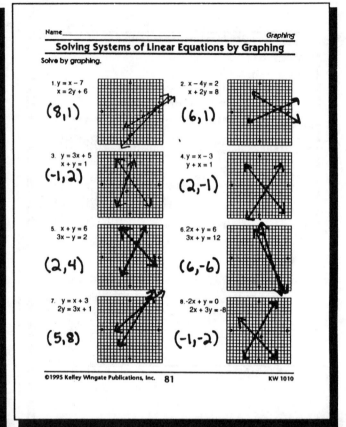

Solving Systems of Linear Equations by Graphing

Solve by graphing.

1. $y = x - 7$
   $x = 2y + 6$
   (8,1)

2. $x - 4y = 2$
   $x + 2y = 8$
   (6,1)

3. $y = 3x + 5$
   $x + y = 1$
   (-1,2)

4. $y = x - 3$
   $y + x = 1$
   (2,-1)

5. $x + y = 6$
   $3x - y = 2$
   (2,4)

6. $2x + y = 6$
   $3x + y = 12$
   (6,-6)

7. $y = x + 3$
   $2y = 3x + 1$
   (5,8)

8. $-2x + y = 0$
   $2x + 3y = -8$
   (-1,-2)

©1995 Kelley Wingate Publications, Inc.   81   KW 1010

Solving Systems of Equations by Addition Method

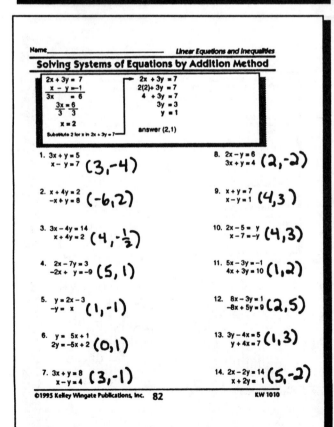

1. $3x + y = 5$
   $x - y = 7$ **(3,-4)**

2. $x + 4y = 2$
   $-x + y = 8$ **(-6,2)**

3. $3x - 4y = 14$
   $x + 4y = 2$ **(4,-½)**

4. $2x - 7y = 3$
   $-2x + y = -9$ **(5,1)**

5. $y = 2x - 3$
   $-y = x$ **(1,-1)**

6. $y = 5x + 1$
   $2y = -5x + 2$ **(0,1)**

7. $3x + y = 8$
   $x - y = 4$ **(3,-1)**

8. $2x - y = 6$
   $3x + y = 4$ **(2,-2)**

9. $x + y = 7$
   $x - y = 1$ **(4,3)**

10. $2x - 5 = y$
    $x - 7 = -y$ **(4,3)**

11. $5x - 3y = -1$
    $4x + 3y = 10$ **(1,2)**

12. $8x - 3y = 1$
    $-8x + 5y = 9$ **(2,5)**

13. $3y - 4x = 5$
    $y + 4x = 7$ **(1,3)**

14. $2x - 2y = 14$
    $x + 2y = 1$ **(5,-2)**

©1995 Kelley Wingate Publications, Inc.   82   KW 1010

Solving Systems of Linear Equations by Multiplication with Addition Method

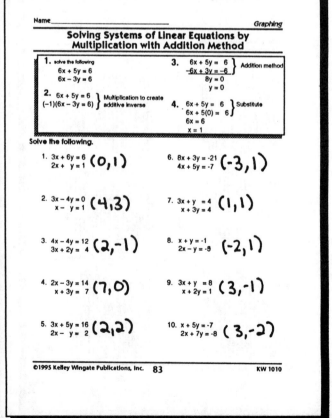

Solve the following.

1. $3x + 6y = 6$
   $2x + y = 1$ **(0,1)**

2. $3x - 4y = 0$
   $x - y = 1$ **(4,3)**

3. $4x - 4y = 12$
   $3x + 2y = 4$ **(2,-1)**

4. $2x - 3y = 14$
   $x + 3y = 7$ **(7,0)**

5. $3x + 5y = 16$
   $2x - y = 2$ **(2,2)**

6. $8x + 3y = -21$
   $4x + 5y = -7$ **(-3,1)**

7. $3x + y = 4$
   $x + 3y = 4$ **(1,1)**

8. $x + y = -1$
   $2x - y = -8$ **(-2,1)**

9. $3x + y = 8$
   $x + 2y = 1$ **(3,-1)**

10. $x + 5y = -7$
    $2x + 7y = -8$ **(3,-2)**

©1995 Kelley Wingate Publications, Inc.   83   KW 1010

© 1996 Kelley Wingate Publications   124   CD-3732

Answer Key

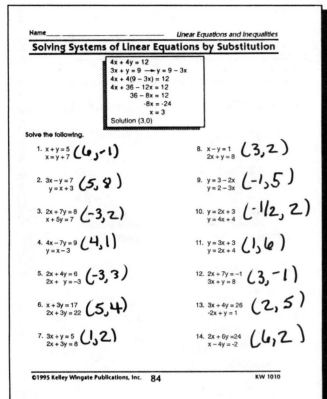

Name_____ *Linear Equations and Inequalities*

Solving Systems of Linear Equations by Substitution

$$4x + 4y = 12$$
$$3x + y = 9 \longrightarrow y = 9 - 3x$$
$$4x + 4(9 - 3x) = 12$$
$$4x + 36 - 12x = 12$$
$$36 - 8x = 12$$
$$-8x = -24$$
$$x = 3$$
Solution (3,0)

Solve the following.

1. $x+y=5$, $x=y+7$ (6,-1)
2. $3x-y=7$, $y=x+3$ (5,8)
3. $2x+7y=8$, $x+5y=7$ (-3,2)
4. $4x-7y=9$, $y=x-3$ (4,1)
5. $2x+4y=6$, $2x+y=-3$ (-3,3)
6. $x+3y=17$, $2x+3y=22$ (5,4)
7. $3x+y=5$, $2x+3y=8$ (1,2)
8. $x-y=1$, $2x+y=8$ (3,2)
9. $y=3-2x$, $y=2-3x$ (-1,5)
10. $y=2x+3$, $y=4x+4$ (-1/2, 2)
11. $y=3x+3$, $y=2x+4$ (1,6)
12. $2x+7y=-1$, $3x+y=8$ (3,-1)
13. $3x+4y=26$, $-2x+y=1$ (2,5)
14. $2x+6y=24$, $x-4y=-2$ (6,2)

©1995 Kelley Wingate Publications, Inc. 84 KW 1010

Name_____ *Radicals*

Simplifying Radicals

$$\sqrt{36x^2y^{18}} = \sqrt{6x^2y^{18}} = 6xy^4$$

Simplify.

1. $\sqrt{x^{16}}$ $x = x^8$
2. $\sqrt{x^8}$ $x = x^4$
3. $\sqrt{x^4y^6}$ x^2y^3
4. $\sqrt{x^5y^5}$ $xy^4\sqrt{xy}$
5. $\sqrt{x^9y^9}$ $x^4y^4\sqrt{xy}$
6. $\sqrt{8x^3}$ $2x\sqrt{2x}$
7. $\sqrt{25x^8y^2}$ $5x^4y$
8. $\sqrt{27x^8}$ $3x^4\sqrt{3}$
9. $\sqrt{54x^9}$ $3x^4\sqrt{6}$
10. $\sqrt{a^{14}}$ a^7
11. $\sqrt{8x^2}$ $2x\sqrt{2}$
12. $\sqrt{81x^6}$ $9x^3$
13. $\sqrt{25x^6}$ $5x^3$
14. $\sqrt{8x^9}$ $2x^4\sqrt{2x}$
15. $\sqrt{64x^9y^{12}}$ $8x^4y^6\sqrt{x}$
16. $\sqrt{9a^4b^8}$ $3a^2b^4$
17. $\sqrt{16x^4}$ $4x^2$
18. $\sqrt{125b^{15}}$ $5b^7\sqrt{5b}$
19. $\sqrt{121y^{12}}$ $11y^6$
20. $\sqrt{x^2y^{10}}$ xy^5

©1995 Kelley Wingate Publications, Inc. 85 KW 1010

Name_____ *Radicals*

Simplifying Radicals

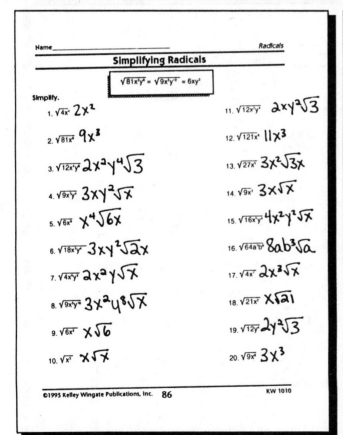

$$\sqrt{81x^6y^6} = \sqrt{9x^2y^{12}} = 6xy^3$$

Simplify.

1. $\sqrt{4x^4}$ $2x^2$
2. $\sqrt{81x^6}$ $9x^3$
3. $\sqrt{12x^4y^8}$ $2x^2y^4\sqrt{3}$
4. $\sqrt{9x^3y^4}$ $3xy^2\sqrt{x}$
5. $\sqrt{6x^8}$ $x^4\sqrt{6x}$
6. $\sqrt{18x^3y^4}$ $3xy^2\sqrt{2x}$
7. $\sqrt{4x^4y^2}$ $2x^2y\sqrt{x}$
8. $\sqrt{9x^4y^{16}}$ $3x^2y^8\sqrt{x}$
9. $\sqrt{6x^2}$ $x\sqrt{6}$
10. $\sqrt{x^3}$ $x\sqrt{x}$
11. $\sqrt{12x^2y^4}$ $2xy^2\sqrt{3}$
12. $\sqrt{121x^6}$ $11x^3$
13. $\sqrt{27x^5}$ $3x^2\sqrt{3x}$
14. $\sqrt{9x^3}$ $3x\sqrt{x}$
15. $\sqrt{16x^4y^5}$ $4x^2y^2\sqrt{x}$
16. $\sqrt{64a^2b^7}$ $8ab^3\sqrt{a}$
17. $\sqrt{4x^7}$ $2x^3\sqrt{x}$
18. $\sqrt{21x^2}$ $x\sqrt{21}$
19. $\sqrt{12y^6}$ $2y^3\sqrt{3}$
20. $\sqrt{9x^6}$ $3x^3$

©1995 Kelley Wingate Publications, Inc. 86 KW 1010

Name_____ *Radicals*

Multiplying Radical Expressions

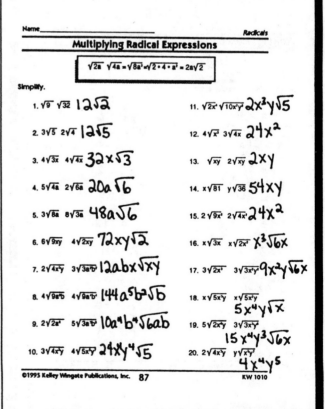

$$\sqrt{2a} \cdot \sqrt{4a} = \sqrt{8a^2} = \sqrt{2 \cdot 4 \cdot a^2} = 2a\sqrt{2}$$

Simplify.

1. $\sqrt{9} \sqrt{32}$ $12\sqrt{2}$
2. $3\sqrt{5} \, 2\sqrt{4}$ $12\sqrt{5}$
3. $4\sqrt{3x} \, 4\sqrt{4x}$ $32x\sqrt{3}$
4. $5\sqrt{4a} \, 2\sqrt{6a}$ $20a\sqrt{6}$
5. $3\sqrt{8a} \, 8\sqrt{3a}$ $48a\sqrt{6}$
6. $6\sqrt{9xy} \, 4\sqrt{2xy}$ $72xy\sqrt{2}$
7. $2\sqrt{4xy} \, 3\sqrt{3a^2b}$ $12abx\sqrt{xy}$
8. $4\sqrt{9a^2b} \, 4\sqrt{9a^2b}$ $144a^5b^2\sqrt{b}$
9. $2\sqrt{2a^2} \, 5\sqrt{3a^3b}$ $10a^4b^4\sqrt{6ab}$
10. $3\sqrt{4xy} \, 4\sqrt{5x^2y}$ $24xy^4\sqrt{5}$
11. $\sqrt{2x} \, \sqrt{10x^2y^2}$ $2x^3y\sqrt{5}$
12. $4\sqrt{x^2} \, 3\sqrt{4x}$ $24x^2$
13. $\sqrt{xy} \, 2\sqrt{xy}$ $2xy$
14. $x\sqrt{81} \, y\sqrt{36}$ $54xy$
15. $2\sqrt{9x^4} \, 2\sqrt{4x^4}$ $24x^2$
16. $x\sqrt{3x} \, x\sqrt{2x^2}$ $x^3\sqrt{6x}$
17. $3\sqrt{2x^3} \, 3\sqrt{3x^2y}$ $9x^2y\sqrt{6x}$
18. $x\sqrt{5x^2y} \, x\sqrt{5x^2y}$ $5x^4y\sqrt{x}$
19. $5\sqrt{2xy} \, 3\sqrt{3xy^2}$ $15x^4y^3\sqrt{6x}$
20. $2\sqrt{4x^2y} \, y\sqrt{x^5y^2}$ $4x^4y^5$

©1995 Kelley Wingate Publications, Inc. 87 KW 1010

Answer Key

Dividing Radical Expressions

Name_____ Radicals

$$\sqrt{\tfrac{12}{3}} = \sqrt{4} = 2 \qquad \sqrt{\tfrac{4}{25}} = \tfrac{\sqrt{4}}{\sqrt{25}} = \tfrac{2}{5}$$

Simplify.

1. $\sqrt{\tfrac{3x^3y^3}{x^2y}}$ $x\sqrt{3y}$

2. $\sqrt{\tfrac{16x}{9x}}$ $\tfrac{4}{3}$

3. $\sqrt{\tfrac{12x^2}{48}}$ $\tfrac{x}{2}$

4. $\sqrt{\tfrac{3x^2}{75y^2}}$ $\tfrac{x}{5y}$

5. $\sqrt{\tfrac{x^2}{25}}$ $\tfrac{x}{5}$

6. $\sqrt{\tfrac{9}{64}}$ $\tfrac{3}{8}$

7. $\sqrt{\tfrac{2(9x^2)}{3}}$ $3x$

8. $\sqrt{\tfrac{12x^2}{3x}}$ $2x$

9. $\sqrt{\tfrac{8x^2}{2x}}$ $2x$

10. $\sqrt{\tfrac{50x^2}{2}}$ $5x$

11. $\sqrt{\tfrac{36x}{25x^3}}$ $\tfrac{6}{5x}$

12. $\sqrt{\tfrac{49}{9}}$ $\tfrac{7}{3}$

13. $\sqrt{\tfrac{4x^2y}{4xy^3}}$ $\tfrac{x}{y}$

14. $\sqrt{\tfrac{2x^2}{18x^4}}$ $\tfrac{1}{3x}$

©1995 Kelley Wingate Publications, Inc.   88   KW 1010

Adding and Subtracting Radical Expressions

Name_____ Radicals

$$2\sqrt{y} + 3\sqrt{y} + \sqrt{y} = 6\sqrt{2} \qquad \sqrt{4x} + 3\sqrt{x} = 2\sqrt{x} + 3\sqrt{x} = 5\sqrt{x}$$

Simplify.

1. $4\sqrt{2x} + 3\sqrt{2x}$ $7x\sqrt{2x}$

2. $3\sqrt{2y} + 2\sqrt{2y}$ $5\sqrt{2y}$

3. $2\sqrt{4x} + 3\sqrt{2x} - 2\sqrt{2x} + 4\sqrt{4x}$ $12\sqrt{x} - \sqrt{2x}$

4. $4\sqrt{x} - 2\sqrt{x} - 3\sqrt{x} + 5\sqrt{x}$ $4\sqrt{x}$

5. $3\sqrt{x^3} + 3\sqrt{x^2}$ $3x\sqrt{x} + 3x$

6. $4\sqrt{y^3} - 2\sqrt{y^3}$ $2y\sqrt{y}$

7. $x\sqrt{x^3} + x\sqrt{x^3}$ $2x^2\sqrt{x}$

8. $3y\sqrt{2y} - y\sqrt{2y}$ $2y\sqrt{2y}$

9. $2\sqrt{50} - 4\sqrt{8} - 3\sqrt{72}$ $-16\sqrt{2}$

10. $2\sqrt{5y} + 4\sqrt{5y} + 3\sqrt{5y}$ $9\sqrt{5y}$

11. $3\sqrt{6x} + 5\sqrt{6x}$ $8\sqrt{6x}$

12. $2\sqrt{y} - 4\sqrt{y}$ $-2\sqrt{y}$

13. $x\sqrt{27} + x\sqrt{12}$ $5x\sqrt{3}$

14. $3\sqrt{x^3} - 4\sqrt{x^3}$ $-x\sqrt{x}$

15. $y\sqrt{y^3} - y\sqrt{y^3}$ 0

16. $x\sqrt{6x} + x\sqrt{24x}$ $3x\sqrt{6x}$

17. $3\sqrt{9x^2y} + 2\sqrt{9x^2y}$ $15xy$

18. $3x\sqrt{4xy} - 5\sqrt{xy}$ $6x^2\sqrt{xy} - 5x\sqrt{xy}$

19. $5\sqrt{24y} + 3\sqrt{54y}$ $19\sqrt{6y}$

20. $3\sqrt{4x^2y} - 8y\sqrt{y}$ $(6x - 8y)\sqrt{y}$

©1995 Kelley Wingate Publications, Inc.   89   KW 1010

Solving Quadratic Equations by Taking Square Roots

Name_____ Radicals

$$x^2 = 36$$
$$\sqrt{x^2} = \sqrt{36}$$ The solutions are 6 and -6
$$x = \pm 6$$

Solve by taking square roots.

1. $x^2 = 9$ $x = \pm 3$

2. $x^2 = 144$ $x = \pm 12$

3. $x^2 - 49 = 0$ $x = \pm 7$

4. $x^2 = 100$ $x = \pm 10$

5. $a^2 - 169 = 0$ $a = \pm 13$

6. $x^2 - 49 = 0$ $x = \pm 7$

7. $a^2 = 196$ $a = \pm 14$

8. $x^2 - 25 = 0$ $x = \pm 5$

9. $x^2 - 81 = 0$ $x = \pm 9$

10. $x^2 - 64 = 0$ $x = \pm 8$

11. $3x^2 - 108 = 0$ $x = \pm 6$

12. $2a^2 - 32 = 0$ $a = \pm 4$

13. $4x^2 - 16 = 0$ $x = \pm 2$

14. $2x^2 - 128 = 0$ $x = \pm 8$

15. $3x^2 - 432 = 0$ $x = \pm 12$

16. $x^2 - 121 = 0$ $x = \pm 11$

17. $3x^2 - 27 = 0$ $x = \pm 3$

18. $5x^2 - 125 = 0$ $x = \pm 5$

19. $x^2 + 81 = 162$ $x = \pm 9$

20. $x^2 - 16 = 0$ $x = \pm 4$

©1995 Kelley Wingate Publications, Inc.   90   CD-3732

Solving Quadratic Equations by Factoring

Name_____ Factoring

$$x^2 - 6x = -9 \qquad x - 3 = 0$$
$$x^2 - 6x + 9 = 0 \qquad x = 3$$
$$(x - 3)(x - 3) = 0 \qquad \text{The solution is 3}$$

Solve by factoring.

1. $x^2 - 4x = 0$ $x(x-4)=0 \; \{0, 4\}$

2. $a^2 - 36 = 0$ $(a+6)(a-6)=0 \; \{-6, 6\}$

3. $y^2 + 9y = 0$ $y(y+9)=0 \; \{0, -9\}$

4. $y^2 + 49y = 0$ $y(y+49)=0 \; \{0, -49\}$

5. $y^2 + 5y - 6 = 0$ $(y+6)(y-1)=0 \; \{-6, 1\}$

6. $y^2 - y - 6 = 0$ $(y-3)(y+2)=0 \; \{3, -2\}$

7. $3u^2 - 12u + 9 = 0$ $3(u-3)(u-1)=0 \; \{3, 1\}$

8. $6x^2 + 12x = 0$ $6x(x+2)=0 \; \{0, -2\}$

9. $x^2 + 7x = 0$ $x(x+7)=0 \; \{0, -7\}$

10. $x^2 + x = x(x + 3)$ $(x+4)(x-2)=0 \; \{-4, 2\}$

11. $y^2 - 8x + 12 = 0$ $(x-6)(x-2)=0 \; \{6, 2\}$

12. $a^2 - 7a = -12$ $(x-3)(x-4)=0 \; \{3, 4\}$

13. $y^2 + 15 = 8y$ $(y-5)(y-3)=0 \; \{5, 3\}$

14. $2x^2 + x = 6$ $(2x-3)(x+2)=0 \; \{\tfrac{3}{2}, -2\}$

15. $5a^2 + 25a = 0$ $5a(a+5)=0 \; \{0, -5\}$

16. $x^2 - 6x + 5 = 0$ $(x-5)(x-1)=0 \; \{5, 1\}$

17. $x - 6 = x(x - 4)$ $(x-2)(x-3)=0 \; \{2, 3\}$

18. $4x^2 + 16x = 0$ $4x(x+4)=0 \; \{0, -4\}$

19. $3x^2 - 9x = 0$ $3x(x-3)=0 \; \{0, 3\}$

20. $x - 25 = x(x - 9)$ $(x-5)^2 \; \{5\}$

©1995 Kelley Wingate Publications, Inc.   91   KW 1010

Answer Key

Worksheet 1 (page 92)

Name_____ Factoring

Solving Quadratic Equations by Factoring

Solve by factoring.

1. $x^2 - 6x + 9 = 0$
$x = 3$

2. $x^2 + 7x + 10 = 0$
$x = -5$ or $x = -2$

3. $x^2 - 4x - 4$
$x = 2$

4. $3x^2 - 13x + 4 = 0$
$x = 1/3$ or $x = 4$

5. $6y^2 - 7y + 2 = 0$
$y = 2/3$ or $y = 1/2$

6. $x^2 - 10x - 25$
$x = -5$

7. $x^2 + 3x - 10 = 0$
$x = -5$ or $x = 2$

8. $r^2 - 15r = 16$
$r = 16$ or $r = -1$

9. $4a^2 + 9a + 2 = 0$
$a = -1/4$ or $a = -2$

10. $2a^2 + a - 6 = 0$
$a = 3/2$ or $a = -2$

11. $4a^2 + 15a - 4 = 0$
$a = 1/4$ or $a = -4$

12. $9x^2 = 18x + 0$
$x = 0$ or $x = 2$

13. $x^2 - 5x + 6 = 0$
$x = 3$ or $x = 2$

14. $2x^2 = 9x + 5$
$x = -1/2$ or $x = 5$

15. $2x^2 - 9x + 9 = 0$
$x = 3/2$ or $x = 3$

16. $6x^2 = 23x + 18$
$x = -2/3$ or $x = 9/2$

17. $3x^2 - 2x - 8 = 0$
$x = -4/3$ or $x = 2$

18. $x^2 = 4x + 5$
$x = 5$ or $x = -1$

19. $a^2 - 6a = 0$
$a = 0$ or $a = 6$

20. $x^2 + 3x - 4 = 0$
$x = -4$ or $x = 1$

21. $x^2 + 7x + 12 = 0$
$x = -4$ or $x = -3$

22. $x^2 + 5x - 6 = 0$
$x = -6$ or $x = 1$

92 KW 1010

Worksheet 2 (page 93)

Name_____ Radicals

Solving Quadratic Equations by Taking Square Roots

$x^2 = 36$
$\sqrt{x^2} = \sqrt{36}$ The solutions are 6 and -6
$x = \pm 6$

Solve by taking square roots.

1. $x^2 = 36$
$x = \pm 6$

2. $x^2 = 16$
$x = \pm 4$

3. $4x^2 - 81 = 0$
$x = \pm 9/2$

4. $x^2 = 64$
$x = \pm 8$

5. $a^2 - 4 = 0$
$a = \pm 2$

6. $9a^2 - 16 = 0$
$a = \pm 4/3$

7. $a^2 = 4$
$a = \pm 2$

8. $x^2 - 36 = 0$
$x = \pm 6$

9. $x^2 - 49 = 0$
$x = \pm 7$

10. $x^2 - 16 = 0$
$x = \pm 4$

11. $3x^2 - 75 = 0$
$x = \pm 5$

12. $3a^2 - 27 = 0$
$a = \pm 3$

13. $3(x + 3)^2 = 27$
$x = 0$ or $x = -6$

14. $(x + 2)^2 = 4$
$x = 0$ or $x = -4$

15. $4(x - 3)^2 = 16$
$x = 5$ or $x = 1$

16. $3x^2 - 48 = 0$
$x = \pm 4$

17. $6x^2 - 54 = 0$
$x = \pm 3$

18. $(x + 1)^2 = 36$
$x = 5$ or $x = -7$

19. $4(x + 2)^2 = 64$
$x = 2$ or $x = -6$

20. $(x + 2)^2 = 36$
$x = 4$ or $x = -8$

93 CD-3732

Worksheet 3 (page 94)

Name_____ Logical Reasoning and

Probability Experiment-Directional Page

Directional Page

Review all terms given on these worksheets and follow the directions below. Answer all questions with your partner.

1. Designate one partner "A" and one partner "B".

2. On your worksheet, calculate the theoretical probability for tossing a fair coin and getting "heads" (H) and "tails" (T). Record these probabilities on the worksheet as directed, changing all fractions to decimals for ease of comparison.

3. Answer questions #1, 2, and 3 on your worksheet now!

4. Get one fair coin from your teacher.

5. "A" flips the coin 10 times while "B" records each outcome as "H" for Heads or "T" for tails.

6. For the next 10 coin flips, "B" flips the coin while "A" records the outcomes.

7. Continue alternating tasks every 10 coin tosses until you have completed 100 coin tosses.

8. Analyze this experimental data to the theoretical probability you calculated earlier.

9. Answer questions # 4 and #5 on the worksheets.

10. There should be a grid on the board to hold all of the experimental data from each cooperative group. Partner "A" should then write their group's experimental data on the board. Class discussion of combined data.

11. After the class discussion of the combined data, refine your answer to question # 5 on worksheet. Write at least two sentences comparing class data to your own experimental data.

Extension Activity: Toss the coin 25, 50, or 100 more times and record the results !!!

***Teacher's note- Each group should receive the following:
1 Directional page
1 Terminology and calculations page
1 Tally sheet
1 Question page
1 Fair coin (penny)

94 KW 1010

Worksheet 4 (page 95)

Name_____ Logical Reasoning and Application

Probability Experiment

Terminology and Calculations Page

Probability is the chance that a given event will occur, expressed mathematically as a ratio from 0 (no chance) to 1 (almost certain)..

Sample Space is the set of all possible outcomes of an event.

Outcomes represent each member of the sample space.

Theoretical Probability is the number of possible outcomes of a given event to the total number of outcomes in the sample space. In other words, theoretical probability is which outcomes will probably occur, given the variable of the situation. We will denote this as P(H) and P(T), for the theoretical probability of "heads" and "tails," respectively.

Sample Space : Fair Coin { }

Calculate:

P(H) = { no. of times H occurs in sample space } = _____ = 0._____
        total no. of outcomes in sample space

P(T) = { no. of times T occurs in sample space } = _____ = 0._____
        total no. of outcomes in sample space

Experimental Probability is the ratio of the frequency of an event to the number of random experiments conducted. We will denote this as P(H) and P(T), for the theoretical probability of "heads" and "tails," respectively.

Use your experimental data to calculate:

P(H) = { No. of heads } = ____ = 0._____   P(T) = { No. of tails } = ____ = 0._____
           10   10   10   10

P(H) = { No. of heads } = ____ = 0._____   P(T) = { No. of tails } = ____ = 0._____
           50   50   50   50

P(H) = { No. of heads } = ____ = 0._____   P(T) = { No. of tails } = ____ = 0._____
          100   100   100   100

95 CD-3732

Answer Key

Name_____ Logical Reasoning and

Probability Experiment

Questions Page

Names_____

As cooperative pairs, answer the following questions.

1. Of what similarly sounding word does "probability" remind you?

Answers will vary.

2. Explain in your own words the difference between theoretical and experimental probabilities.

↓

3. What predictions (conjectures) can you make about the results of your experiment based on the theoretical probability of tossing "heads" or "tails"? In other words what do you think will happen when you toss a coin 10, 50 , and 100 times and analyze the results.

↓

4. Analyze the results of your experiment. Does your experimental probability confirm or contradict your original predictions about the likelihood of tossing a fair coin and getting "heads" or "tails"?

↓

5. Make a statement about the relationship between experimental and theoretical probabilities of a given event based on your experiment.

|

©1995 Kelley Wingate Publications, Inc.   96   KW 1010

Name_____ Logical Reasoning and

Probability Experiment

Tally sheet

Names_____

Write an H or T next to each number as the coin is flipped. Record the total number of H's or T's per ten coin flips in the end column.

Key: H=Heads   T=Tails

										H	T
1	2	3	4	5	6	7	8	9	10		
11	12	13	14	15	16	17	18	19	20		
21	22	23	24	25	26	27	21	29	30		
31	32	33	34	35	36	37	38	39	40		
41	42	43	44	45	46	47	48	49	50		
51	52	53	54	55	56	57	58	59	60		
61	62	63	64	65	66	67	68	69	70		
71	72	73	74	75	76	77	78	79	80		
81	82	83	84	85	86	87	88	89	90		
91	92	93	94	95	96	97	98	99	100		

©1995 Kelley Wingate Publications, Inc.   97   KW 1010

Great Success!

earns this award for

_____

I am Proud of You!

_____

Signed

Date

Great Job!

Receives this award for

Keep up the great work!

Signed

Date

Keep up the Great Work!

_____

earns this award for

_____

You are TERRIFIC!

_____
Signed

_____
Date

You Did It!

_____

earns this award for

_____

Keep Up The Great Work!

_____
Signed

_____
Date

$$\left(\frac{x^2}{y^3}\right)^4$$

$$\frac{15x^3}{3x}$$

$$x^2 \cdot x \cdot x \cdot x^2$$

$$x^3 \cdot x^3 \cdot x^3$$

$$(x^2y^3)^2$$

$$\frac{x^{14}}{x^3}$$

$$7x^{-8}$$

$$(-2)^{-3}$$

$$\left(\frac{4}{5}\right)^{-2}$$

$$\frac{x^7 \cdot x^5}{x^3}$$

$$(7x^{-3})^2$$

$$(-9x^3)^{-2}$$

$$(2xy)^{-1}$$

$$(2x^3)(3x^4)$$

$$(3x)^4$$

$$(2x^2y)^3$$

$$\frac{x^8}{y^{12}} \qquad x^4y^6 \qquad \frac{25}{16} \qquad \frac{1}{2xy}$$

$$5x^2 \qquad x^{11} \qquad x^9 \qquad 6x^7$$

$$x^6 \qquad \frac{7}{x^8} \qquad \frac{49}{x^6} \qquad 81x^4$$

$$x^9 \qquad \frac{1}{-8} \qquad \frac{1}{81x^6} \qquad 8x^6y^3$$

$(-3)^3$

$x \cdot x^2 \cdot x^3$

$(5x^2)^2$

$x^8 \cdot x^{-10}$

$\dfrac{x^8}{x^3}$

$(x^3)^4$

$(x^9)^3$

$(4x)^{-4}$

$x^3 \cdot x^2$

$\left(\dfrac{2}{3}\right)^{-2}$

$x^5 \cdot x^{-4}$

$4x^{-4}$

2^{-4}

$5x^{-2}$

$(x^7)^2$

$x^7 \cdot x^8 \cdot x^{-3}$

-27

x^6

$25x^4$

$\dfrac{1}{x^2}$

x^5

x^{12}

x^{27}

$\dfrac{1}{256x^4}$

x^5

$\dfrac{9}{4}$

x^{10}

$\dfrac{4}{x^4}$

$\dfrac{1}{16}$

$\dfrac{5}{x^2}$

x^{14}

x^{12}

Factor: $72x^2 + 9x + 18$

Factor: $9 - 3y$

Factor: $2x + 5x^2$

Factor: $7x + 14y$

Factor: $100 - x^2$

Factor: $4x^2 - 25$

Factor: $x^2 - 9$

Factor: $5x^2 + 125$

Factor: $16x^2 - y^2$

Factor: $49x^2 + 81y^2$

Factor: $81x^2 - 121$

Factor: $x^2 - 1$

Factor: $x^2 - 5x - 6$

Factor: $x^2 - 8x - 15$

Factor: $7x^2 - 28$

Factor: $2x^2 - 50$

$9(8x^2+x+2)$ $3(3-y)$ $x(2+5x)$ $7(x+2y)$

$(10+x)(10-x)$ $(2x+5)(2x-5)$ $(x+3)(x-3)$ $5(x^2+25)$

$(4x+y)(4x-y)$ prime $(9x+11)(9x-11)$ $(x+1)(x-1)$

$(x+2)(x+3)$ $(x+3)(x+5)$ $7(x+2)(x-2)$ $2(x+5)(x-5)$

Factor:

$x^2 + 15x + 56$

Factor:

$x^2 + 12x + 11$

Factor:

$x^2 - 7x + 12$

Factor:

$x^2 - 17x + 72$

Factor:

$x^2 - 10x + 21$

Factor:

$x^2 + 9x + 20$

Factor:

$x^2 - 2x - 8$

Factor:

$x^2 - x - 42$

Factor:

$x^2 - 7x - 18$

Factor:

$x^2 - 7x - 8$

Factor:

$x^2 + 3x - 28$

Factor:

$x^2 + 3x - 4$

Factor:

$x^2 + x - 20$

Factor:

$x^2 - 7x - 44$

Factor:

$2x^4 - 32$

Factor:

$3x^2 - 6x - 72$

$(x-8)(x-9)$ $(x-3)(x-4)$ $(x+1)(x+11)$ $(x+7)(x+8)$

$(x-7)(x+6)$ $(x+2)(x-4)$ $(x+5)(x+4)$ $(x-3)(x-7)$

$(x+4)(x-1)$ $(x+7)(x-4)$ $(x-8)(x+1)$ $(x-9)(x+2)$

$3(x-6)(x+4)$ $2(x+2)(x-2)(x^2+4)$ $(x-11)(x+4)$ $(x+5)(x-4)$

$\sqrt{49}$	$\sqrt{121}$	$\sqrt{4x^2}$	$\sqrt{16}$
$\sqrt{x^9}$	$\sqrt{x^6}$	$\sqrt{169x^4}$	$\sqrt{144}$
$\sqrt{x^8}$	$\sqrt{72}$	$\sqrt{200}$	$\sqrt{8}$
$\sqrt{25}$	$\sqrt{64}$	$\sqrt{1}$	$\sqrt{27}$

± 7

$\pm x^4\sqrt{x}$

$\pm x^4$

± 5

± 11

$\pm x^3$

$\pm 6\sqrt{2}$

± 8

$\pm 2x$

$\pm 13x^2$

$\pm 10\sqrt{2}$

± 1

± 4

± 12

$\pm 2\sqrt{2}$

$\pm 3\sqrt{3}$

$$\frac{2x}{3} = 24$$

$$x - 8 = -2$$

$$7 - x = 8$$

$$2x - 3 = 13$$

$$2x + 3 = 13$$

$$-4x + -3 = 17$$

$$x + 5 = -4$$

$$x - 7 = -2$$

$$x - 4 = -8$$

$$\frac{x}{3} = -9$$

$$x - 5 = 8$$

$$x + 3 = -11$$

$$x + 7 = -8$$

$$5x - 7 = -12$$

$$x + 3 = -5$$

$$-5x = 30$$

x = 36

x = 5

x = -4

x = -15

x = 6

x = -5

x = -27

x = -1

x = -1

x = -9

x = 13

x = -8

x = 8

x = 5

x = -14

x = -6